Men and Battle
Decision at Sea: The Convoy Escorts

DECISION AT SEA:

A Talisman / Parrish Book

THE CONVOY ESCORTS

Peter Kemp

Elsevier-Dutton
New York

ISBN: 0-525-93004-3

Published in the United States by E. P. Dutton,
a Division of Sequoia-Elsevier Publishing Company, Inc., New York
Published simultaneously in Canada by
Clarke, Irwin & Company Limited, Toronto and Vancouver

Art Direction: The Etheredges
Production Manager: Stephen Konopka

Printed in the U.S.A.   First Edition
10 9 8 7 6 5 4 3 2 1

Contents

Preface

The writing of this book has brought back many memories of the savage battle fought mainly in the wide wastes of the Atlantic throughout the five and a half years of World War II, the battle which alone held the key to the ultimate Allied victory. But memory alone is no true basis on which to write a book which depends so much on detailed facts of events that occurred more than 30 years ago, and I have to thank David Brown, head of the Naval Historical Branch of the Ministry of Defence, London, and his staff for giving me access to contemporary convoy records and reports, and to the Naval Staff History, *Defeat of the Enemy Attack on Shipping*, which was compiled entirely from the official records of the British and German navies. For the U.S. Navy's part in this great battle I have relied mainly on Rear Admiral Samuel Eliot Morison's semiofficial *History of United States Naval Operations in World War II*, and for that of Canada on G. N. Tucker's official history, *The Naval Service of Canada*. Others to whom my thanks are due, mainly for many past conversations and notes on the campaign, are Vice-Admiral Sir Peter Gretton, Captain Donald Macintyre—both notable escort group commanders during the war—and Patrick

Beesly, who was a colleague of mine in the U-boat Tracking Room in the Admiralty throughout the long campaign. To them all I owe much, though I would stress that all the comments and opinions expressed in this book are entirely my own.

PETER KEMP

1. The First Blow

Early in the morning of 22 August 1939, 17 oceangoing U-boats sailed from their German bases into the North Sea. Proceeding submerged throughout daylight hours, only surfacing after dark to recharge their batteries, they made their way up the coast of Norway, then headed westward through the gap between the Shetland and the Faeroe Islands out into the Atlantic. Once there, they were to take up prearranged waiting positions on a line stretching southward from west of the Hebrides down toward Gibraltar. On receipt of word from U-boat headquarters that war against Britain and France was imminent, they were to leave their waiting positions and move into their operational ones, 60 miles to the south. They had strict instructions to conduct submarine warfare in accordance with the German naval prize laws. Before any merchant ship was sunk she was to be challenged, and her passengers and crew seen into her lifeboats before any torpedoes were fired. These orders were in accordance with the articles of the Hague Convention, which Germany had accepted and signed in 1930.

One of these 17 submarines was *U-30*, commanded by Oberleutnant Fritz-Julius Lemp. Lemp's war operational area extended between latitudes 54° and 57° North and longitudes 12° to 19° West, an area of 180 miles by 200 miles in the Northwest Approaches to Britain. For seven days

Lifeboats quickly became a symbol of the Atlantic battle

he remained in his waiting position until, on 3 September, he received the signal informing him that Britain and Germany were at war. Now he moved down into his operational area.

At noon on 1 September the Donaldson Atlantic Line's passenger ship *Athenia* had sailed from Prince's Dock on the Clyde, at Glasgow, bound for Montreal. She was a liner of 13,581 tons, built in 1923, and had gained such a reputation among her regular passengers as a comfortable "family" ship that many of them preferred her to any other liner. She was commanded by Captain James Cook; this was to be his 14th crossing of the Atlantic as her captain. On board were 420 passengers and a crew of 315. The *Athenia* was bound first to Belfast to pick up another 136 passengers, and then to Liverpool, where a further 546 passengers were waiting to come on board. All were embarked by 4:30 P.M. on 2 September, and the *Athenia* set sail for Canada. She passed Inishtrahull, off the northwestern corner of Ireland, the last point of European land to be sighted, at 4:30 A.M. on 3 September, and was well out into the Atlantic by 11 o'clock, when news of the declaration of war against Germany was received by radio.

Her passenger accommodation on this voyage was uncomfortably crowded. The growing realization during the past two or three weeks that Europe was drifting inevitably into war had caused the withdrawal of several liners from their normal passenger service, some for fitting out as

troopships—Cunard's *Queen Mary* was one of these—others for conversion
into armed merchant cruisers. Still others had simply been taken out of
service until the international situation had cleared sufficiently for their future employment to become known. All this had created an intense de-
mand for accommodation on the ships which were still being kept in passenger service—mainly from American and Canadian citizens anxious to
get home before the gathering war clouds burst into storm. When the
Athenia was leaving Glasgow, the dockside was crowded with Canadians
and Americans who had hoped for a last-minute chance of a berth on
board.

As the ship left behind her the last sight of Europe and steamed out
into the Atlantic, she had on board a total of 1,102 passengers, of whom 469
were Canadian and 311 were United States citizens. She also carried 155
refugees from central Europe, mainly families from Germany, Poland and
Czechoslovakia who had managed to get out before being struck by the
Nazi terror. The remaining 167 passengers were British and Irish. More
than three-quarters of the total were women and children.

When the announcement of the declaration of war was received on
board the *Athenia*, Captain Cook ordered all the 26 lifeboats and 21 life
rafts to be fully prepared for any emergency, and all passengers on board
were asked to attend a second lifeboat drill. They had already attended an
obligatory drill shortly after the ship had sailed. And in accordance with in-

3

structions already issued by the British Admiralty in anticipation of war, the ship was made ready for being darkened at sunset, with her scuttles blacked out and her navigation lights dimmed.

About 200 miles out in the Atlantic *U-30* was proceeding south from her waiting area into her operational area. She was submerged, creeping forward at about three knots and waiting for sunset when she could come to the surface to recharge her batteries and, incidentally, greatly extend her range of vision. To the east of her was the *Athenia*, making her best speed of 16 knots and steering a little north of her normal course to Canada in accordance with diversionary instructions received from Naval Control under the general direction of the Trade Division of the British Admiralty.

The sun set shortly after 7 o'clock, and *U-30* surfaced to begin her battery charge and freshen the air in the boat. There was still nearly an hour of twilight to come, and Lemp welcomed the opportunity to sight a possible foe before full darkness fell. Like all young commanding officers in wartime, he was eager to strike an early blow for his country.

Less than 10 miles away the *Athenia*, still steaming at 16 knots, darkened ship. Lemp sighted her as she approached and noted that *U-30* was in a favorable position for attacking. He could see the *Athenia* clearly enough to recognize that she was a liner, and he noted that instead of the usual blaze of light that normally distinguished liners at sea during the hours of darkness, her scuttles had been blacked out and she was burning dimmed navigation lights. His orders forbade him to sink merchant ships at sight, especially passenger ships, but what if this large liner approaching him was an armed merchant cruiser? If she were, she would undoubtedly be a legitimate target. The fact that she had darkened ship seemed to him suspicious.

It was time for *U-30* to dive, for the *Athenia* was approaching fast. According to his later testimony, Lemp still had not decided what she was as he peered through *U-30*'s periscope and maneuvered his submarine into an attacking position. When his periscope sight came on, the temptation to claim his first victim so early in the war became too great to resist. Convincing himself that the ship he was watching was an armed merchant cruiser, he fired all four of *U-30*'s bow tubes at her. Two of his torpedoes missed. One got caught up in its tube. But the fourth hit the liner abreast the engine room bulkhead and exploded. The time was 7:39 P.M., with half an hour of twilight still left.

The masthead lookout in the *Athenia* saw the white tracks of the torpedoes in the water as they approached the ship and shouted a warning to the bridge. It was too late to try to avoid them. They were traveling at 40 knots and were only 250 yards away when they were first sighted. A few of the passengers and some of the crew were killed outright when the torpedo exploded against the ship's side. Others were disabled with broken bones and other injuries. But none of the lifeboats were damaged, and Captain

4

Admiral Dönitz, directing brain of the U-boat fleet

Cook was hopeful that they could be lowered with most of the passengers and crew safely in them. He ordered the *Athenia* to be abandoned. He also drafted the appropriate wartime distress signal: "SSSS SSSS SSSS *Athenia* GFDM [the *Athenia*'s international designation] torpedoed 56 42 N, 14 05 W."

The call was picked up by the Norwegian tanker *Knute Nelson*, 40 miles away; by the Swedish yacht *Southern Cross*, about 55 miles away; and by the U.S. freighter *City of Flint*, 200 miles away. All three made for the *Athenia*'s position at their best speed. The signal was also heard by the naval wireless stations in Britain, and three destroyers—the *Escort*, the *Electra* and the *Fame*—were ordered to close the *Athenia* at full speed. Another vessel that read the distress call was *U-30*, and Lemp, when he learned the name of the ship he had torpedoed, knew he was in deep trouble for so flagrant a disobedience of the Führer's orders.

The *Athenia* took a long time to sink and most of her lifeboats got clear of her, though some shipped a considerable amount of water as they were lowered. As often happens in such cases, some passengers missed their footing in trying to get aboard the boats and were thrown into the sea. One lifeboat overturned as it was lowered into the sea, dumping its occupants into the water. Another was smashed later by the propellers of the *Knute Nelson* as it was drawn under her stern when attempting to come alongside. Nevertheless, 1,305 passengers and crew were rescued by the *Knute Nelson*, *Southern Cross*, *Escort* and *Electra*, though four of them died later of their injuries. Those who perished numbered 112, of whom 93 were passengers and 19 crew. Of the passengers who lost their lives, 69 were women and 16 were children.

The news of the sinking of the *Athenia* caused consternation in Germany. It was at once reported to Hitler, who gave orders for broadcasting to the world an immediate denial that the sinking was caused by a German U-boat. Lemp had not, as he should have done, reported the attack by radio, and there may have been some legitimate doubt at first as to whether a U-boat had been responsible. The entry in the War Diary of the German Naval Staff for noon on 4 September 1939 reads, "The torpedoing of the *Athenia* by a German submarine is to be rejected definitely as a British atrocity report. Even the most northerly of our submarines cannot have been in this area, as the northern boundary of its area of operations lies 70 miles further south. This *Lusitania* incident is probably an attempt by Great Britain to draw America into the war. Discussion to this effect with the Führer's staff. The State Secretary of the Foreign Office issues a definite denial." Nevertheless, Hitler ordered a signal to be sent immediately to all U-boats at sea: "By order of the Führer, on no account are operations to be carried out against passenger steamers, even when under escort."

The German denial, broadcast to the world, reached ridiculous heights. "If the *Athenia* had actually been torpedoed," ran the German broadcast, "this could only have been done by an English submarine. We believe the present chief of the British Navy, Churchill, capable of even that crime . . . There is also the possibility that Churchill had a little bomb blown up inside."

The news of the sinking also caused consternation in Britain. It was at once taken as evidence that Germany intended to wage unrestricted submarine warfare at sea irrespective of her being a signatory of the Hague Convention. It appeared to be on a par with all the other international promises made by Hitler during the years before the war, promises which had been regularly ignored when there could be profit in the breaking of them. The British had not thought that unrestricted submarine warfare would be adopted from the start of the war, although the possibility of its gradual introduction had been taken into account in the general war plans. No one knew better than the Royal Navy itself how unprepared it was for this new and unexpected dimension of the war at sea. It implied the full and immediate introduction of a complete and integrated Atlantic convoy system, even though there were not nearly enough escort vessels with the necessary long-range endurance. It meant that for the first two or three years of war, Atlantic convoy would have to be something of a

"A bitter and savage fight to the death . . ."

patchwork affair, until an accelerated wartime building program could produce long-range escorts in the huge numbers required for so vast an operation. Inevitably, a lot of merchant ships were going to be sunk, a lot of lives were going to be lost, before the U-boats in the Atlantic could be mastered. The sinking of the *Athenia* on the first day did not present a happy prospect to Britain as the war at sea swept steadily into its stride.

U-30 returned to Wilhelmshaven on 26 September, and Admiral Karl Dönitz, commander of the U-boat fleet, was waiting on the quay. As soon as Dönitz knew the truth he sent Lemp by air to report to the Naval High Command in Berlin, where he was seen by Admiral Raeder, Commander in Chief of the Navy. But it was too late now to retract the original denial, and too late to order a court-martial of Lemp, since such a trial could not have been kept secret. On his return to Wilhelmshaven, Lemp was placed temporarily under cabin arrest, but as there was to be no court-martial he had to be released, and he was able to resume his career as a U-boat captain. All that remained to be done to maintain the German denial was to remove the incriminating page in *U-30*'s official log and replace it with a forged one that made no mention of the *Athenia* and indicated that *U-30* was not even near the position from which she had attacked. The fiction was maintained throughout the war, and it was only in 1945 that the German Navy at last admitted the truth.

Lemp's torpedo which hit and sank the *Athenia* was not the first one fired in the war. Four minutes after the declaration of war a U-boat in the North Sea fired four torpedoes at the British submarine *Spearfish* as she was proceeding to her war station. All four missed their target. But Lemp's torpedo was the first one fired in what was to become known as the Battle of the Atlantic, and its success in sinking the *Athenia* made it the herald of five and a half years of a bitter and savage fight to the death in the wide wastes of the oceans, in which no quarter was given, or indeed expected, by either side.

2. The Convoy Method

The safeguarding of merchant shipping by convoy is one of the oldest operations of naval war. It dates back at least to the 13th century, when ships carrying wine to England from the English possessions in southwestern France were defended on their passage by armed ships belonging to the English King. Because it was successful in the wine trade, the practice of convoy was rapidly extended to cover almost all merchant shipping in times of war—timber, pitch and tar from the Baltic states, tea and spices from the East, even the annual flota of treasure ships from the New World to Spain in the 16th century. So successful was convoy as a method of safely transporting merchandise across the seas in times of war that during the 18th-century wars between Britain and France, convoy was made compulsory for all British merchantmen, and owners and masters were heavily fined if their ships sailed out of convoy or if they deserted a convoy once their voyage had started.

With so great a background of historical experience it was strange that Britain, at the time the world's leading naval power, turned her back on the principle during the first great world war of the 20th century. There were times in 1916 and 1917 when the country teetered on the brink of starvation and defeat. Dependent, as an island nation, upon imported food and munitions, raw material for manufacturing, and oil and machine tools, Britain lived or died on her ability to bring her merchant ships loaded with these supplies safely across the oceans. It was one of the fundamental elements of her existence as a nation at war, a strategic pattern of war proven by more than four centuries of naval battle. In the end, a return to the successful policy of all earlier wars saved Britain from disaster, and the practice of convoy once again came into its own as the only means of defense against a systematic enemy attack on merchant shipping.

This departure from sound and proven naval practice had cost Britain 2,480 ships of 7,759,090 tons (out of an Allied total of 5,531 ships of 12,850,814 tons) lost by enemy action, and the lives of 14,721 merchant seamen and fishermen. The ships could be replaced by new construction, but the men were gone forever, scattered across the floors of the oceans where their ships were sunk. There are, of course, losses of merchant ships in every war, convoy or no convoy, but the losses in the final year of that war, when convoy had been built up to cover more than 90 percent of ocean trade, were at least tolerable in comparison with the deadly years before when the merchant ships had sailed unguarded.

The public revulsion to war and slaughter after 1918 was perhaps a main cause of the failure of the British Admiralty to analyze the results of the German attack on shipping. There was much wishful thinking that unrestricted submarine warfare could be banned by international agreement and, on the material side, that the appearance of the sound-detection device called asdic (now known as sonar) would make all submarine warfare unproductive. Both hopes were doomed to disappointment. Unrestricted submarine warfare was much too valuable a weapon against an enemy whose existence depended on seaborne supply; no belligerent opposed to such an enemy would ever discard it, no matter what world opinion might think of unseen attack against innocent merchant ships. And sonar, in spite of all the high hopes which had attended its introduction, had a number of serious limitations. It had a minimum and maximum range of detection, the maximum being around 1,500 yards in good working conditions. Neither bearings nor ranges could be read accurately, and a possible error of up to 25 yards in range—when the killing radius of a depth charge was no more than seven yards—was not good enough. It also was rarely possible to discriminate between submarine and nonsubmarine echoes. The sonar of that day could not detect a submarine on the surface, and in rough weather and in waters with steep temperature gradients its performance fell off considerably.

Nevertheless, although all this was well enough known, the euphoria persisted. In Britain the Shipping Defence Advisory Committee, the government committee charged with the protection of shipping in war, was told by the Admiralty: "The submarine menace will never be what it was before. We have means of countering a submarine which are very effective

Convoy would have to prove its value again

and which will normally reduce our losses from that weapon. It will never be a fatal menace again as it was in the last war."

On the other side of the hill the forces for the next onslaught were gathering. Although under the terms of the Treaty of Versailles Germany was forbidden to build submarines, she used the years between 1922 and the coming to power of Hitler to keep abreast of submarine development by setting up a small foreign undercover organization and maintaining a secret U-boat technical section. In 1933, when Hitler came to power, the construction of U-boats was begun. In 1935, Hitler broadcast to the world his repudiation of the disarmament clauses of the Treaty of Versailles, and a few weeks later a naval treaty was discussed between Great Britain and Germany, one of its clauses allowing Germany to build a submarine fleet of a tonnage equal to that of Great Britain's. Germany, however, agreed not to exceed 45 percent of the British submarine tonnage for the time being, without further discussion, and also agreed, under certain conditions, not to torpedo merchant ships at sight. These were promises which had been heard before, and they had been broken under the reality of war. The naval treaty was signed on 18 June 1935, but the first German U-boat built since the end of the war slid down the stocks two days before the signing.

It seems odd, looking back at those last years of peace which separated the two world wars of the 20th century, that the British Admiralty still could not make up its mind about the value of convoy in wartime. In

1914-18 there could have been no more startling vindication of its efficacy than the results that followed its belated introduction in 1917. The adoption of convoy proved to be the turning point of the war. Now in 1935 the same enemy had given notice to Britain that she would once again rely upon the U-boat as her main weapon in any sea war. Yet in this same year the British Parliament was informed that the Admiralty did not intend to introduce convoy on the outbreak of war. Two years later the message was that the Admiralty did "not anticipate any use of the convoy system" when submarine and aircraft attack were restricted but might introduce it if international law were violated. In March 1938 the annual naval estimates were reduced by deferring the building of 16 destroyers, two escort vessels and three patrol vessels, all of which were valuable for the protection of merchant ships. And almost at the same time the Admiralty reversed its policy for the defense of shipping. It expressed the view that "the institution of a convoy system wholly or in part may be necessary from the outbreak of war."

But by now it was too late. No plans existed for a ship designed as a convoy antisubmarine escort and suitable for production under an accelerated wartime building program. This was still the case when, on 29 April 1939, Hitler denounced the naval treaty he had signed with Britain in 1935. It was certain now that he was intent on war and that his main naval weapon was to be the U-boat. During July and August the Admiralty ordered 56 patrol vessels for escort purposes, mainly because of the threat of air attack against coastal shipping. As there were no specific designs available for the purpose, they decided to build small ships of a modified whale-catcher type, and because the patterns were in existence, these ships were to be fitted with a four-cylinder, triple-expansion engine used in a whaler. These engines produced a speed of 14 to 15 knots, hardly remarkable in view of the 18½-knot surface speed of the U-boats they were designed to catch. In the actual experience of wartime convoy these new small escort ships were found to be almost useless in winter, partly because of their excessive rolling in a seaway—which exhausted their crews—and partly because of their lack of maneuverability. They were known as the Flower-class corvettes, and 56 were ordered under the 1939 building program.

About the same time a class of small destroyers, known as the Hunt class, were being built, but their production was slow because of a lack of suitable building yards. They were designed mainly as escort destroyers for fast warships, but also with an eye to filling the gap in convoy escorts. They proved to be unsatisfactory in ocean service, chiefly because of a lack of endurance.

When war was declared on 3 September 1939, there were about 180 vessels in the Royal Navy fitted with sonar. Nearly 150 of these were destroyers, most of them earmarked for service with the Home and Mediterra-

12

nean Fleets. The remaining 30 were coastal patrol vessels and sloops, the latter having proved unable to withstand the winter gales in the North Atlantic. It was certain, therefore, that for the first two years of war, until the building of new escort ships could get into its stride, the protection of trade convoys would be spread very thin indeed.

If the war came too early for Britain to build up an adequate escort force, it also came too early for Germany. A long-term plan for building a balanced fleet had been worked out in Germany, based on Hitler's promise that there would be no war in Europe before 1944. The German fleet would by then comprise 13 battleships, 33 cruisers, 4 aircraft carriers, a large number of destroyers and 250 U-boats. As all these would have been new ships, they would have provided a formidable threat to the aging fleets of Britain and France, particularly because the surface warships would, like the U-boats, be directed mainly against the Allied seaborne trade. When war was declared some four years earlier than Hitler had predicted, the German Navy consisted of the 2 battle cruisers *Scharnhorst* and *Gneisenau*, 3 "pocket battleships," 1 heavy and 5 light cruisers, 17 destroyers and 57 U-boats, of which 48 were operational, the remainder either refitting, undergoing trials or earmarked for training.

In addition to the U-boats that sailed for their war operational areas in the last days of August 1939, two pocket battleships were also sent out, one to operate as a commerce raider in the North Atlantic, the other in the South Atlantic. Then, on the first day of the war, Oberleutnant Lemp in *U-30* sank the liner *Athenia*, striking the first blow in what was to become known as the Battle of the Atlantic. This was to be a struggle that endured from the first day of the war to the last, the longest and most savage underwater battle of all recorded naval history.

The quick loss of the *Athenia* shattered any hopes there might have been in Britain that the German U-boats would exercise some discretion in their attacks on unarmed and undefended ships, as they were supposed to do under the international treaties to which Germany was a signatory. It was of course unknown in Britain that Oberleutnant Lemp had exceeded his orders in sinking the *Athenia*; the fact of the sinking had to be accepted as evidence of future German intentions. Nor was it known in Britain that Hitler had ordered his U-boats and pocket battleships to observe the rules of sea warfare laid down in the Hague Convention (the order had not been issued in any spirit of humanity or altruism but purely in the hope that, after Poland had been crushed in the initial onslaught, Britain and France would agree to make peace). Already there had been too much evidence of Hitler's frailty in the keeping of international promises for Britain to accept the stream of German protestations that the sinking of the *Athenia* was not a deliberate act. There was no choice but to accept the evidence of the fact that the *Athenia* had been sunk without warning by a U-boat. So, in the Atlantic at least, it was to be a war to the death.

14

③. The Happy Time

It took the British some time to organize the full convoy system to which the sinking of the *Athenia* had committed them. The first convoys to be set up were those carrying troops across the English Channel to France and those up and down the east coast between the Thames and the Firth of Forth. The troop convoys were always escorted by destroyers; the coastal convoys, by ships with good antiaircraft as well as antisubmarine armament, because the main threat in English coastal waters was expected to come from German air attack.

Outward-bound ocean convoys were begun four days after the declaration of war. They were known as OA, if sailing from the port of Southend, and OB, if sailing from Liverpool. When they were clear of the Irish coast, the southbound ships were separated into OG convoys to Gibraltar, the ships bound to North America remaining in their OA and OB convoys. Homeward-bound ocean convoys began on 14 September with one from Sierra Leone, in west Africa, and the first of the convoys from Halifax, Nova Scotia, given the identity letters HX, sailed on 16 September. This began the famous series of HX convoys around which the Battle of the Atlantic was to be most fiercely fought, a long, groping campaign waged without mercy by day and by night in the wide waters of the North Atlantic—a campaign on which was to depend the whole outcome of the war in Europe.

From the first day of the ocean convoy sailings the limitations of the British escort forces were exposed: the penalty resulting from the peacetime failure to design and build suitable escort vessels had to be paid. Because of the limited endurance of their escorts, outward-bound ocean convoys could be escorted, at best, only as far as 15° West longitude—about 200 miles out into the Atlantic—and there the escorts waited to bring incoming convoys in to Liverpool or Plymouth. After reaching the limit of escort, the outward-bound convoys were expected to retain their formation for the next 24 hours, even though unescorted, before dispersing and sailing independently to their destinations. Homeward-bound convoys leaving Halifax were escorted by local Canadian escort vessels as far as 56° West longitude, but because they were usually carrying essential war supplies and also because German surface raiders were known to be at large in the Atlantic, they were given an ocean escort of one of the older battleships or an armed merchant cruiser. Neither type of ship was fitted with antisubmarine equipment, nor did either carry any form of antisubmarine weapon. They were there purely to guard against attack by a surface raider.

Such an attack came in the autumn of 1940, when convoy HX-84, having parted from her Canadian antisubmarine escort, was being guarded across the Atlantic by the armed merchant cruiser *Jervis Bay*. The German pocket battleship *Admiral Scheer* had earlier evaded British air reconnaissance patrols flown across the North Sea and, completely unobserved, reached the Atlantic through the Denmark Strait. Her first victim was an independently routed merchant ship, which failed to send out a raider report before she was sunk. The lack of such a report was, in fact, a direct threat to the convoy, for had one been received there would have been just enough time to change course and avoid the danger area. That same evening the *Jervis Bay* sighted a large ship to the southward, quickly identified her as a pocket battleship, reported her presence by wireless and steamed toward her to do battle, ordering the convoy to make smoke and scatter to the northward. It was bound to be a most unequal battle, for the *Jervis Bay*, like all armed merchant cruisers, had only five elderly 6-inch guns to pit against the six 11-inch and eight 5.9-inch guns of the *Scheer*. Yet Captain Edward Fogarty Fegen, in command of the *Jervis Bay*, gained enough time by his action for most of the 37 ships in the convoy to escape in the gathering darkness. After the armed merchant cruiser had been sunk, as was inevitable, the *Scheer* could find only five ships of the convoy to attack. Captain Fegen was awarded a posthumous Victoria Cross for his gallant action and self-sacrifice, and it is pleasant to record that, later that evening, one of the merchant ships in the convoy returned to the scene of the action and rescued some of the survivors from the *Jervis Bay*. This kind of action grew to be typical, lifting this grim battle of the oceans to new heights of courage. It was no light matter to risk a ship in dangerous waters to bring

Fog turns this escort's neighbor into a ghost ship

help and survival to unfortunate men whose own ships had been sent to the
bottom by enemy attack.

The *Scheer*'s attack on HX-84 brought another remarkable story of
courage and endurance to set beside that of the *Jervis Bay*. One of the
merchant ships attacked by the *Scheer* after the sinking of the *Jervis Bay*
was the *San Demetrio*, a small tanker loaded with 10,000 tons of oil. Her
navigating bridge was almost completely blown away by gunfire, her hull
was holed in several places and the oil in one of her tanks set on fire. The
crew abandoned ship in the ship's three lifeboats, for it seemed certain that
the rest of her cargo would explode and tear her apart. The lifeboats got
separated in the heavy sea, and the following morning one of them, carrying the second officer, the chief engineer and 13 men, sighted smoke on
the horizon. Hopefully, they rowed toward it, but as they closed in they
recognized their own ship, the *San Demetrio*, still burning. She was surrounded by a pool of flaming oil, but by noon the following day this fire had
burned itself out and the lifeboat was able to come alongside the ship. The
tanker was still burning aft and the deck amidships was red hot, but the
men were able to get aboard over the bows. Much of the engine machinery
had been damaged by blast from the *Scheer*'s shells, but after six hours'
work the chief engineer succeeded in getting steam to the main engines
and the *San Demetrio* began to move again. With the restored steam pressure it was now possible also to get water pressure in the fire main, and
two hours later the worst of the fires were put out.

A U-boat approaches the German battle cruiser *Scharnhorst*

So the battered *San Demetrio* started for home with a skeleton crew of one officer, one engineer and 13 men, facing a long voyage of over 1,000 miles across an ocean in which the U-boats roamed. All her navigating instruments—compass, charts, steering gear, wireless—had been lost in the wreckage of the bridge. Navigating by the sun by day and by the stars by night, Arthur Hawkins, the second officer, brought the ship safely home to port with the greater part of her cargo intact.

This sort of attack, however, was unusual; in general, the German surface raiders did not attack convoys. They found their prey among the independent merchant vessels which still sailed unescorted or which straggled from a convoy and were no longer under protection. In February 1941, when the battle cruisers *Scharnhorst* and *Gneisenau* were at sea in the North Atlantic on a raiding operation, they sighted south of Greenland the masts of an eastbound convoy, HX-106, which they expected to be unescorted, or at best escorted only by an armed merchant cruiser. The two German ships separated in order to attack from opposite directions simultaneously, but as they closed for the kill they discovered that the convoy was being escorted by the old British battleship *Ramillies*, a veteran of the First World War. Acting together, the battle cruisers could probably have blown the *Ramillies* out of the water and and sunk some of the merchant ships as well, but they both retired at high speed without firing a shot.

They had better luck 14 days later, when they sighted the smoke of a number of ships which, having passed the limit of antisubmarine escort, were dispersing to continue their voyages independently to North American ports. Five of them totaling 25,784 tons, were sunk, but since several had got off raider reports on their wireless, Admiral Lütjens, commanding the two battle cruisers, broke off the attack. The *Scharnhorst* and the *Gneisenau* steamed down to the South Atlantic, hoping to find an unescorted convoy to add to their bag. On 8 March a homeward-bound convoy from Freetown, Sierra Leone—SL-67—was sighted, but like HX-106, it was being escorted by a battleship—this one the *Malaya*, a veteran of the Battle of Jutland in 1916. Lütjens therefore retired without attempting an attack and returned to the North Atlantic and the more profitable Halifax route. Here he had a real stroke of good fortune, finding 16 ships recently dispersed from outward-bound convoys and sailing independently. All were sunk, 82,000 tons of merchant shipping being added to Lütjens's total of destruction. Some of the survivors were picked up by the British battleship *Rodney*, which reached the area too late to engage the German ships. The *Scharnhorst* and the *Gneisenau* were now ordered to return to the French Biscay port of Brest, there to await an even bigger operation which Admiral Raeder, the German Commander in Chief, was planning.

And there they waited while the bigger plan was hatched and then went awry. They were damaged by systematic bombing as they lay in the Brest dockyard. And Admiral Raeder's master plan, which was to form a squadron with the battle cruisers and the new battleship *Bismarck*, together with the heavy cruiser *Prinz Eugen*, to operate in the Atlantic and close that ocean to all merchant shipping, fell into ruins when the *Bismark* was sunk by the British Home Fleet on her maiden voyage into the Atlantic. In the final event, the *Gneisenau* never again operated against merchant shipping, being damaged beyond repair in a bombing raid on Kiel, and the *Scharnhorst* met her death in the icy waters of the Arctic Ocean when she next attempted to interfere with a convoy, from which in fact she was driven away before she could fire a shot.

In the first months of the war, the U-boats—like the surface raiders—rarely attacked convoys, finding their victims in the main among the independently routed ships and in the stragglers unable, or sometimes unwilling, to keep their positions in a convoy. Only ships capable of steaming between 9 and 14.9 knots were included in convoys, and during the first few months neutral ships were excluded, in the belief that Germany would not want openly to antagonize nations not yet at war. Ships with a speed of less than 9 knots and of 15 knots and over were sailed independently—the slow ships because they would inevitably hold up the progress of a convoy, the fast because they were difficult to hit with a torpedo unless a U-boat had the good fortune to sight them far enough ahead of their course to reach a firing position in time. Otherwise they had the speed to outrun a

U-boat. Many of the slow ships—and some of the fast ones, too—gave to the U-boats their early taste of blood.

The months of July to October 1940 were what the U-boat captains were later to call their "happy time," when the U-boat aces won fame by the number of ships they sank and the aggregate of tonnage they sent to the bottom. Germany rang with their names—Prien, Endrass, Kretschmer, Frauenheim, Schepke—and German propaganda broadcasts to England gloated over their mastery of the art of sinking merchant ships. They achieved their successes mainly against independent ships and stragglers, but had no hesitation in attacking convoys when they sighted them, realizing how inadequately defended they were. Those were the months when the average size of escort fell below two, and many quite large convoys, of 40 ships or more, were sent out guarded only by a single escort vessel. Also in the U-boats' favor was the limiting distance of convoy, some 200–250 miles out into the Atlantic. It was easy enough for submarines to operate beyond this limit, where they knew that the convoys went completely unguarded.

During these unhappy four months the U-boats sank 217 ships, 144 of them sailing independently and 73 in convoys. The total tonnage lost was 872,719 tons—a sad blow to British hopes of containing the merchant shipping toll within tolerable bounds. Equally depressing was the realization that these heavy sinkings had been achieved by relatively few U-boats on patrol, for as yet the U-boat strength at sea during these months had not even caught up the level deployed on the first day of war. What was later to become known as the "exchange rate"—U-boats destroyed for merchant ship tonnage sunk—was equally disappointing, for only six U-boats had been killed during this holocaust.

In Germany too, the early months of the war were a disappointment to Admiral Dönitz, who commanded the U-boat force. He started the war with 57 U-boats, of which 48 were operational, and of these 30 were small boats of 250 tons, suitable for use in the North Sea and British coastal waters only. On the first day of the war, the day on which the liner *Athenia* was sunk, 17 oceangoing U-boats were at sea, but the total dropped fairly rapidly as the boats came in at the end of their patrols. Nor did it reach that number again until September 1940, when the overall U-boat strength again reached 57, new U-boats completed and added to the fleet being exactly offset by the number of U-boats sunk. But by then the big expansion program put in hand on the outbreak of war was beginning to take effect. And as the numbers steadily grew, Admiral Dönitz was enabled to bring in new tactics in attack which he had designed and tried out in exercises in the Baltic before the war. These tactics were introduced to circumvent the sonar device, on which so much reliance had been placed in Britain, and in this they were completely successful. Dönitz's methods heralded the direct attacks on convoys which were the prominent feature of 1941 and 1942,

U-boat commander Erich Topp, a 1940 ace

Oil tanker goes up like a seagoing torch

years in which the slaughter of merchant ships reached proportions so vast that the whole outcome of the war hung in the balance.

Even by the end of 1940 there was no doubt in the minds of the leaders on both sides of the struggle that the war would be won and lost in the Atlantic. Dönitz had calculated that if Germany could inflict a monthly loss of 700,000 tons of Allied shipping, of which his U-boats would have to account for the lion's share, the war in Europe would be won by Germany. This was probably an overestimate; most likely, 600,000 tons of shipping a month would have turned the trick. This was the figure calculated by the British Admiralty as the maximum which could be sustained if the Allied cause were to prosper, and even with that rate of loss there would be no hope of building up war supplies sufficient to mount a return to Europe, the final battlefield on which the war had to be won. Control of the Atlantic was, for both sides, the key to ultimate victory.

Behind the actual scenes of conflict in the oceans, so to speak, both sides were organizing hard for what was to prove a battle to the death. In Germany, Dönitz personally took entire charge of all operations of his U-boats, setting up a highly sophisticated headquarters from which he could control the movements of every individual U-boat in the Atlantic. Such an organization required a very high degree of control by wireless signals and called for a considerable volume of reports from U-boats on station in the Atlantic, giving their positions, the state of the weather, sightings of indi-

22

vidual ships and convoys, the consumption of fuel on board, the number of torpedoes remaining and so on. Every tiny bit of information, significant or not, was all grist to Dönitz's mill, giving him a complete and detailed daily picture of every happening in the Atlantic battle.

It was on this huge volume of daily signals from the U-boats that the British antisubmarine organization was at first largely built. The Admiralty in London was an operational naval headquarters (unlike the War Office and Air Ministry, which did not control operations of the Army and Air Force) in daily radio communication with ships at sea, and inside it was set up the U-boat Tracking Room. Radio direction-finding stations were built along the whole length of the coastline of Britain, and later in many places overseas. From these a bearing of every wireless signal was taken and signaled to the Admiralty, where they were plotted on charts in the U-boat Tracking Room. These bearings, when plotted, gave a submarine's position, and thus the general disposition of the U-boat fleet in the Atlantic became known. When enough U-boat signals were received, it became possible to warn the convoy escorts of the dangers ahead, and often to reroute convoys at sea clear of the known or suspected concentrations of U-boats. A great many ships owed their lives to this daily game of hide-and-seek.

As the war developed, even more valuable information became available to both sides. First in the time scale came the work of the German B-dienst, the cryptographers engaged in attacking the British naval code, into which all important naval operational signals were enciphered. This code became vulnerable soon after the start of the war. The administrative naval code had been used so extensively by the British Mediterranean Fleet during the Ethiopian crisis of 1935–36 that the German cryptographers had been able to intercept a huge volume of signals on which to work. This administrative code had given the Germans a useful lead into the operational code, and by 1940 a good deal of decoded information was being fed into the German U-boat headquarters. Later, from the beginning of 1942 to the middle of 1943, the B-dienst was able to supply Dönitz, almost daily, with priceless information. Included among the decrypts was the daily convoy signal, which gave not only the position, course and speed of all convoys at sea but also the estimated position of all U-boats. It was a winning position in the Atlantic battle, and it was held until June 1943, when the British realized what was happening and changed their code.

Later in the war the Allied side was enabled to enjoy the same advantage, when its cryptographers at last broke through the intricacies of the now-famous Enigma machine on which the German signals were enciphered. The first tentative breaks came in 1941, though they were too spasmodic to be of very much assistance. This was because the settings of the machine were changed every 24 hours, which virtually required the breaking of a new cipher every day. But with growing knowledge of, and practice in, the German system of using the cipher machine, British cryp-

23

tographers succeeded in mastering the Enigma, and throughout the last two and a half years of the war the German naval cipher was read almost continuously. The value of information gained from this source was incalculable.

The scientists, too, worked hard behind the scenes of the Atlantic battle. For the first three years of the war, the antisubmarine weapons available to the British escort ships were little advanced on those developed in World War I. Depth charges were still discharged from throwers fixed to fire on the beam and from chutes over the stern, making it inevitable that sonar contact with a U-boat was lost well before an attack could be made. The only means of illumination at night was still the star shell, a most unsatisfactory method because it provided light only briefly. These were the first problems to be tackled by British scientists, who eventually came up with the answers—the ahead-firing depth-charge mortars, which enabled contact with a submerged U-boat to be held right up to the moment of attack, and Snowflake, a powerful rocket flare that virtually turned night into day. The development of shortwave radar and of shipborne wireless direction-finding was another enormously important contribution made by scientists to the winning of the Battle of the Atlantic.

Scientists were equally active behind the German scene. They improved the German torpedo and its firing pistol, making it a reliable and predictable weapon where at the start of the war it had missed more often than it had hit because of deep running and premature explosion. They also developed electric torpedoes, which left no track in the water, and torpedoes which homed themselves onto the sound of a ship's propellers. They developed an entirely new design of submarine, the Walter U-boat, which employed a closed-cycle turbine engine for use when submerged. The engine gave an underwater speed of over 20 knots, unheard of at that stage of submarine development. Fortunately for the Allies, the Walter boat arrived just too late. When shortwave radar began to be fitted in the Allied escort vessels, German scientists brought out a search receiver for U-boats which registered the radar pulses and told a U-boat captain that an enemy was in contact so that he could dive out of harm's way. All these scientific advances, of course, were gradual as the campaign developed, but they indicate the volume of effort which was devoted on both sides to the winning of this vital battle.

By the end of 1940, the U-boats had sunk 2,607,314 tons of Allied and neutral shipping out of total losses from all causes of 4,747,033 tons, roughly 55 percent. This was a long way short of the 700,000 tons a month which Dönitz reckoned necessary for a German victory, and well short too of the similar British calculation of 600,000 tons. But by the end of 1940 the construction of U-boats started at the outbreak of the war was beginning to become operational. Dönitz could now count on a steady monthly growth in the number of submarines available for the attack on shipping. The increase would enable him to start his new tactics, with which he expected vastly to enlarge the tonnage his U-boats could send to the bottom. The crux of the Atlantic battle was about to arrive, and the struggle was to sway backward and forward between the two sides for two and a half years before a final verdict could be given.

4. Atlantic Alliance

In April 1940 Hitler struck at Denmark and Norway, occupying the first with no opposition and overrunning the second within six weeks. Even before the whole of Norway was in his hands, he struck again, this time attacking the Netherlands, Belgium and France. In another six weeks German forces were in occupation of eastern France down to the border with Switzerland, and they controlled all of the Biscay coast.

So far as the Atlantic convoys were concerned, these were devastating blows. They gave to Germany a number of well-defended and well-equipped ports which not only effectively outflanked the British strategic position but also provided the U-boat fleet with new bases which very considerably lessened the distances they had to sail to reach their patrol areas in the Atlantic. With Trondheim and Bergen in Norway, and Lorient and La Pallice in the Bay of Biscay, U-boats were able to cut down their voyage times to their operational areas by several days, which in its turn gave them that many extra days on patrol. Moreover, it was much more difficult now to try to attack U-boats while they were on passage to their operational areas, for these new bases led directly into open waters where submarines virtually became needles in haystacks.

It was fortunate for Britain that, even by the beginning of 1941, the

German submarine leaves its base in northern Norway

German U-boat building program had not yet got into its swing. After various vicissitudes, mainly caused by Hitler's unwillingness to give priority to the U-boat's requirements for steel, the new program had been settled at 25 submarines a month. In July 1940, with Norwegian and French bases now in his hands, Hitler lifted all his restrictions on U-boat building, but by then it was too late in the day to expect a rapid increase. Although the number of operational U-boats certainly grew throughout 1941, it did not yet reach a decisive level—certainly not the level which Dönitz needed in order to introduce his new tactical plan, under which his U-boats would hunt and destroy in groups—the "wolf-pack" theory. This tactic lay still in the future, but even before it became possible Dönitz had another ace or two up his sleeve.

The admiral was, above all, a dedicated submariner. He had commanded U-boats during World War I and had seen how the introduction of a convoy system by Britain in 1917 had saved the country from almost certain defeat. He had spent the years between the two world wars trying to devise schemes of beating the convoys, confident that the time would come when Germany and Britain would once again be at war. Dönitz was a complete realist, and unlike most contemporary submariners he looked upon the U-boat as a surface ship able to dive beneath the surface, rather than as a submerged vessel able to come to the surface at will. In his philosophy of submarine warfare he therefore considered that a submarine should attack on the surface whenever possible, using its undoubted physical advantages to do so. The two main surface-attack advantages were a very small silhouette, almost invisible in darkness, and a relatively high speed compared with that of the ships being attacked. Both of these assets were lost when a submarine dived.

So Dönitz laid his plans for 1941 while still waiting for the big build-up in numbers that would enable him to introduce his wolf-pack attacks. For the time being it was to be the individual attack on the surface at night. It would be up to the U-boat commander to seize the initiative and take full advantage of the fact that a surfaced U-boat could only be spotted with great difficulty in the darkness and was at the same time completely immune from detection by the escorts' sonar sets.

It was a system which inevitably produced a few captains whose brilliance in individual attack built them up into heroes based on the amount of merchant ship tonnage they had sent to the bottom. It was not so very difficult a thing to do in 1939 and 1940, when the convoy system was still getting under way and there were plenty of independently routed ships, and others that straggled from their convoys, to swell their totals. And it was by no means difficult in 1941 to sink ships in the convoys themselves, because the escort building program was only just starting, so far as the bigger frigates were concerned, and the existing corvettes, which had to bear most of the burden, were too small and too slow to take a proper toll of the attacking U-boats. And there were still not enough of them to provide a strong escort force for every ocean convoy.

The three greatest U-boat aces at the start of 1941 were Günther Prien, who had leapt into fame in 1939 when he took his submarine into Scapa Flow and sank the old battleship *Royal Oak;* Otto Kretschmer; and Joachim Schepke. Each of them had been decorated by Hitler with the Knight's Cross and Oak Leaf for having sunk more than 200,000 tons of shipping; in fact, Schepke had been credited with 230,000 tons, Prien with 245,000 tons and Kretschmer with a mammoth 282,000 tons. They had each perfected Dönitz's tactic of the surfaced attack at night. They would shadow a convoy during the daytime from astern and beyond the visibility range of the escort force, their surface speed being ample for them to keep up with the convoy, and then still on the surface close in during the dark hours when with their tiny silhouette they were almost invisible, penetrating the escort screen and actually mingling with the merchant ships in the convoy. Once there, they had few problems. Their targets were so close that they could hardly miss with their torpedoes; they were still virtually invisible; and if they were sighted and attacked, they could dive and hope to get clear, knowing that the escorts could not afford to indulge in a long sonar hunt while the convoy they were guarding was steaming away in the distance. It was not, perhaps, quite as easy as during the "happy time" of 1940, as there were fewer independent ships on the oceans, but it was still not difficult.

Heavy weather forced U-boats to dive

There were the occasional respites when the Atlantic weather was too bad even for the U-boats to operate in. That these conditions were even more uncomfortable in the corvettes, which formed the bulk of the ocean escorts, goes without saying, for they were terrible sea boats in rough weather and, in the words of a contemporary saying, would "roll their guts out on wet grass." But an Atlantic gale usually forced the U-boats to dive. Otherwise the high seas would drive solid over their bridges, and they might ship too much water down their conning-tower hatches. And once below the surface they could see little through the mountainous Atlantic waves, and in any case were too slow when submerged to keep up with a convoy. So heavy weather in the Atlantic was welcomed by the convoys and their escorts. Even the discomfort of life in a wildly plunging corvette and the attendant anxieties of trying to keep a convoy in station and properly closed up during a prolonged gale were infinitely preferable to a savage night attack by U-boats.

There were 10 days in January 1941 when the Atlantic weather brought such a respite to the convoys, and the U-boat total of sinkings dropped well below the monthly average of 1940. February, too, was a wild month in the Atlantic, and though the submarines did better—39 ships of 196,783 tons, compared with the January total of 21 ships of 126,782 tons—the performance was not nearly good enough to win the Atlantic victory. But March was, in a way, a turning point in the battle.

U-boats sank 41 ships of 243,020 tons, but they lost five of their number in doing so, about one-fifth of their operational U-boat fleet at that time.

On 7 and 8 March, Convoy OB-293 was heavily attacked, and two of the escorting corvettes (*Camellia* and *Arbutus*) and the World War I destroyer *Wolverine* sank *U-70* and *U-47*. Ten days later Convoy HX-112 was similarly attacked; the destroyers *Walker* and *Vanoc* sank *U-99* and *U-100*. Later in the same month the antisubmarine trawler *Visenda* sank *U-551*. This was good going in the state of the Atlantic battle at the time, better indeed than was then realized in Britain—for the captain of *U-47* was Günther Prien, of *U-99* Otto Kretschmer and of *U-100* Joachim Schepke, the three great heroes of the U-boat fleet. Prien and Schepke were both killed; Kretschmer was captured and spent the remaining years of the war as a prisoner. The captain of HMS *Walker*, the victor of the battle with *U-99*, was Commander Donald Macintyre, who was to become one of the most experienced escort group commanders in the Western Approaches Command and a notable killer of U-boats. This ending of their wartime U-boat careers, within the space of 10 days, marked the close of the period of individual brilliance, with all that it had meant in inspiration to their fellow U-boat captains. Without such men to lead the attacks, Admiral Dönitz was forced to plan them from his headquarters ashore, taking upon himself all detailed organization and actual tactical command of the U-boats at sea. No longer was it enough for him to bring the U-boats to the convoys and leave the rest to the enterprise of individual captains. The loss of these three aces signaled the start of the wolf-pack tactics, though only in a modified form until the supply of new U-boats was great enough to swamp the defense.

But it was not only the submarines that were causing the losses. Almost as destructive in the attack on the ocean convoys were aircraft. Coastal convoys were being punished both by aircraft and by the new magnetic mines. The east and south coast convoys round the shores of Britain were within easy range of the new German airfields in occupied Holland, Belgium and France, particularly along the east coast, where they were restricted to a relatively narrow route inside the British defensive minefield. Here it was easy for aircraft continually to drop mines along the convoy route and in the approaches to the main ports. These coastal convoys were free from the menace of the U-boats, which always disliked operating in the shallow waters of the North Sea, but the dive-bomber and the mine proved to be almost as deadly an enemy. By 1941 most merchant ships on these routes were defensively armed with antiaircraft guns, but the targets were never easy to hit, and the toll of sinkings by aircraft bombs remained high. It took a high degree of courage on the part of the seamen manning these merchant ships to keep the convoys running to a regular timetable when they could see for themselves the almost daily loss of some of their mates from mine and bomb.

The ocean convoys, at least for their first three or four days outward bound and for the same period inward bound, suffered from the same plague. At the start of the war the Germans had developed the four-engine Focke-Wulf 200 Condor, a civilian aircraft, into a long-range reconnaissance bomber. In July 1940 they had been able to base squadrons of these planes at Bordeaux, on the Biscay coast, and at Stavanger in Norway. With their long endurance they could range hundreds of miles out into the Atlantic, where they could sight and shadow a convoy, reporting its position, course and speed back to U-boat headquarters. A convoy which, during the course of its voyage, saw a Focke-Wulf overhead could reckon on a subsequent attack from U-boats as soon as they had been summoned to the scene. The Focke-Wulf could also home in shore-based bombers to the convoy, as well as attack with its own bombs. Throughout 1940 Condors accounted for 192 ships with a total tonnage of over 580,000.

In February 1941 the German admirals convinced Hitler that if the war against Britain was to be won it would have to be won at sea, and on the 6th of that month the Führer directed that all German striking power, air as well as sea, was to be turned against the Allied overseas supply systems. That meant shipping, and the air effort against the convoys was

FW 200 Condor patrol bomber flies over a freighter just before it is torpedoed

doubled. During 1941 air strikes against shipping caused the loss of 371 ships of more than a million total tons, nearly half the tonnage sunk by U-boats.

The growing threat to ships from the air brought in due course its countermeasures. The defensive arming of merchant ships certainly had a considerable moral effect on their crews—at least they could fire back at their tormentors, even if it had little effect in discouraging them. A more promising line of defense was the development of the CAM ship, the catapult aircraft merchant ship. It carried a single Hurricane fighter, which, on the appearance of a Focke-Wulf, was catapulted into the air, in the hope of shooting the German aircraft down or at least driving it away. On completion of the mission the pilot parachuted into the sea; the hope was that he would be close enough to an escort to be picked up. The Hurricane, of course, was ditched. There were some CAM ship successes—for instance, a Hurricane from the CAM ship *Maplin* shot down a Focke-Wulf 400 miles out to sea in August 1940—but the disadvantages of the method were that the fighter could fly only one mission, and the recovery of the pilot was problematical. More than one of these gallant men found that they made

Canadian escort vessel, the corvette *Dawson*

their landing in the middle of a convoy, where there was the danger of their parachute's fouling the propellers of a merchant ship and dragging them under to their death.

From the CAM ship was developed the MAC ship, the merchant aircraft carrier, a much more promising answer to the problem. Basically it involved the building of a flight deck about 400 feet long above the upperworks of a suitably large merchant vessel, usually a tanker or a grain ship. The MAC ship could carry six fighters, and they could land on the flying deck after their flights and be used again and again.

The first ship to be converted into a MAC ship was the captured German merchantman *Hannover*. She carried six American Martlet fighters and was renamed HMS *Audacity*. She had her first success in September 1941 during a heavy U-boat attack on Convoy OG-74, outward bound to Gibraltar, when one of her fighters shot down a Focke-Wulf that was shadowing the convoy. She was included in the escort force of the next homeward convoy from Gibraltar, which had been delayed until a really strong escort could be assembled to fight it through a heavy concentration of U-boats off the Straits of Gibraltar. In command of the escort force was Commander F. J. Walker, who was to become almost a legendary figure in the Atlantic in the years ahead and whom we shall meet again as the convoy story unfolds.

The convoy sailed on 14 December, and on the 15th the Australian destroyer *Nestor* sank *U-127* off Cape St. Vincent. Next day the convoy was sighted and reported by a Focke-Wulf, and Dönitz ordered nine U-boats in the vicinity to close in and attack. By 17 December the convoy was beyond the range of shore-based air cover from Gibraltar, and the Martlets of the *Audacity* had to take over. Two Focke-Wulfs were shot down, and a Martlet assisted in the sinking of *U-131*. In all, five U-boats and two merchant ships out of the convoy were sunk during this battle, though there were also serious losses among the escorts. One destroyer was sunk, a sloop was damaged when she rammed and sank a U-boat, and the *Audacity* was torpedoed and sunk while operating her aircraft outside the escort screen. Nevertheless, it was a distinct victory over the U-boats, almost the first notable one since the start of the war. When Dönitz called off the attack after sending in three more submarines, he was quick to note the danger which the *Audacity* had posed to his entire campaign and gave orders to his captains that the destruction of any aircraft carrier seen with a convoy was always to be the first objective of an attack.

Of all the enemies which a submarine may face, the one the submarine captain dislikes most is the aircraft. Even though at this stage of the war there was no weapon carried by an aircraft capable of destroying a submarine, the mere presence of an airplane overhead forced the submarine to dive and therefore to lose contact with her prey. It was the *Audacity*'s aircraft which were responsible for the fact that nine U-boats, and later three more, could only sink two merchant ships during a seven-day battle. They kept the U-boats submerged during the day so that they fell far astern of the convoy, and when any of them came to the surface to try to catch the convoy and keep in contact, an aircraft sighted and reported her to the escorts.

The *Audacity* was the first fruit of an Admiralty dream. Because of the lack of endurance of most shore-based aircraft in 1941, and the lack of availability of such long-range aircraft as were in existence because of the prior claim of the RAF's Bomber Command, the British Admiralty had been working on the assumption that convoys would have to provide their own antisubmarine air patrols throughout their voyages. This could only come about if a small carrier could be included in the escort force. Even before the *Audacity* had become operational, another five suitable merchant ships had been earmarked for conversion into MAC ships, and the United States was asked for six small escort carriers, to be built under lend-lease. But this, naturally, had to be a fairly long-term project, and it would certainly be well into 1942 before these carriers could arrive and be worked up into operational efficiency. In fact, their arrival and working-up in Great Britain coincided almost exactly with the Anglo-American landings in North Africa in November 1942, and many of them had to be used in escorting the troop and supply convoys needed to sustain that massive attack. The others were more urgently needed in the Arctic, where the convoys were within range of German shore-based bombers. The Atlantic convoys had to wait until the invasion of North Africa was successfully concluded before they could gain the immense benefit of continuous air escort throughout their ocean passages. In the final analysis it was just this continuous air escort that proved to be the decisive factor in winning the Battle of the Atlantic.

Yet there were some positive factors, even in 1941, in the Atlantic battle, though there was still bound to be a very long and painful road ahead. Hitler's invasion and occupation of Denmark in April 1940 had drawn attention to the position of the Faeroe Islands and Iceland, both of them Danish possessions, and Britain was quickly on the scene to prevent a German takeover of the islands along with the mainland. Iceland was by far the more important in the context of the Battle of the Atlantic. Placed as it was more or less halfway along the convoy route between Halifax and Liverpool, it offered a unique strategic advantage. Adequate harbors capable of development as refueling bases, and the construction of airfields that could handle long-range aircraft, meant that the convoys need no longer steam for a large part of their passage without any escort at all. As the war had developed, the limit of ocean convoy had been gradually creeping further out into the Atlantic. The first limit had been about 200 miles west of Ireland, at which point the outward-bound convoys had had to make the remainder of their voyage on their own while their escorts switched to a homeward-bound convoy. A few months later this limit was pushed out another 100 miles, and by April 1941, with the facilities of Iceland now in operation, some convoys could be escorted halfway across the Atlantic before their escorts had to leave them to refuel in Iceland. But the main objective had always been the provision of antisubmarine surface escort right across the Atlantic, which required the development of bases in eastern Canada and Newfoundland, as well as in Iceland. More crucial still was the availability of an adequate number of escort vessels with efficiently trained crews. By mid-1941 the emergency building programs put in hand both at home and in Canada at the start of the war were beginning to bear fruit. Corvettes were joining the Navy in increasing numbers, were being formed into escort groups and, after a period of intensive training both as individual ships and together as a group, were being sent out on the convoy routes. With escort groups operating from each end of the Atlantic and using Iceland to refuel, it was at last possible to provide the full, continuous surface antisubmarine escort which the convoys desperately needed. The first convoy to enjoy this new measure of protection was HX-129, which sailed from Halifax on 27 May 1941.

While this solution of the problem was being found in the Atlantic, other less happy preoccupations were emerging. The German attack on the Soviet Union in June 1941 had opened up a new theater of war, with all its demands for continuous supplies of war materials of every description. Russia was tremendously hard pressed during the initial German advance; many of her main areas of production were overrun. In her desperation she called on Britain and the United States to make good her losses and to increase her powers of resistance by large and regular shipments of tanks, aircraft and other weapons of war. British and American naval authorities met on several occasions during the summer and autumn to coordinate convoy routes, communications, escort strengths and other basic elements that go with the formation of a full convoy system. But the Soviets could not be kept waiting while all the essential details were worked out. The first shipment of Hurricane fighters was made before regular convoys began, and the system was properly introduced when Convoy PQ-1 left Hvalfjord in Iceland on 29 September, bound for Archangel.

The only possible supply route to Russia was by sea through the Arctic Ocean, a distance of 1,500 to 2,000 miles, depending on the ports of departure and arrival and the ice conditions in the Arctic. These Arctic convoys were a commitment of the British Home Fleet and called for escorts of cruisers and destroyers. As there was no possibility of a refueling base along this barren ice-swept route, every convoy had to be accompanied by an oiler so that the escorting ships could refuel at sea. PQ (outward) and QP (homeward) convoys operated on a 10-day cycle. Since it took about three weeks for the escorts to make the round trip to Murmansk, and longer if the port of destination was Archangel, the calls on the Home Fleet for escorts were exceptionally heavy. Nevertheless, it was a burden that had to be accepted. There could be no let-up. This famous series of convoys began quietly enough, but as soon as Germany came to realize the

35

huge volume of supplies that was reaching Russia along this sea route, her reaction was intense and savage. Since she controlled the whole length of the Norwegian coast up to the North Cape, with its many secure ports and anchorages, and there was a relatively narrow gap of sea between the North Cape and the edge of the Arctic ice through which the convoys had to pass, the task of attacking the convoys was not difficult. All the ships had to pass within easy range of U-boats based in northern Norway and of torpedo bomber squadrons based even closer to the convoy route. The attacks ultimately rose in a crescendo of fury, and the great convoy battles which ensued had to be fought out in the most inhospitable waters in the world. But at this early stage these bitter battles still lay in the future, though by the end of 1941 Germany was concentrating destroyers and U-boats in increasing numbers in northern Norway, and there was no one who could be unaware of what those moves foretold for the months that lay ahead.

Although it happened at the other end of the world, the Japanese attack on the U.S. Pacific Fleet in Pearl Harbor on 7 December 1941 had a profound effect on both sides in the Atlantic battle. The Japanese onslaught automatically brought the United States into the war, and Admiral Dönitz

German submarine skipper on patrol in Arctic waters

was quick to recognize that there would be rich pickings for his captains off the American eastern seaboard, one of the great sea traffic lanes of the world. Moreover, it was a traffic lane of exceptional importance to the Allies, for along it sailed tankers carrying oil from Venezuela and the Netherlands East Indies; a regular supply of oil was vital to the whole prosecution of the war. Dönitz wasted no time in sending six of his largest U-boats into the area and ordering another six of the Atlantic submarines to leave their existing patrol areas off Greenland and Newfoundland and concentrate for an all-out assault on the east coast of America. By the end of the year they were all on their way.

The effect of the American entry into the war was, on the British and Canadian antisubmarine forces in the Atlantic, largely psychological at first. There was a feeling of welcome relief that they would no longer be fighting the U-boats alone in the Atlantic, that they now had a committed participant behind them taking the place hitherto occupied by a well-wishing friend. In the months before Pearl Harbor the United States had taken many concrete steps in showing with which side her sympathies lay. Lend-lease had become law in March 1941, and its first fruits were the transfer to Britain of 10 Coast Guard cutters to swell the long-range escort groups operating on the Sierra Leone convoy route. Air bases were opened in Greenland and Bermuda, and the leased naval base at Argentia, in Newfoundland, was activated. An American Marine brigade arrived in Iceland to relieve the British garrison and assume "police observation" duties over the waters between the United States and Iceland, which meant in effect that American naval forces would be convoying the steady stream of American merchant shipping to and from Iceland. As yet these naval forces were not allowed to escort British convoys but, so to speak, their foot was in the door.

The door was opened wider in September 1941, when Western Hemisphere Defense Plan Number 4, agreed to by Winston Churchill and President Roosevelt in their August meeting off Argentia, was implemented. Under this plan German surface raiders attacking shipping in the waters between the United States and Iceland were to be engaged by American naval forces, and, more important, U.S. warships were allowed to escort convoys comprising ships not of American registry while Canadian warships could escort merchant ships flying the American flag.

This had been a huge step forward, and from mid-September American destroyers were to be seen escorting some of the HX convoys to a meeting point in the mid-Atlantic, where Liverpool-based escort groups took the convoys over. But with U-boats operating off Cape Race, in the Straits of Belle Isle, and off southern Greenland, it was inevitable that sooner or later they would tangle with American escorts. The first encounter came in September 1941, when the U.S. destroyer *Greer* was attacked by *U-652* and replied with depth charges. During the following

37

month the destroyer *Kearney* was torpedoed by a U-boat, and the destroyer *Reuben James* was sunk while escorting Convoy HX-156.

But after Pearl Harbor it was war, and no longer an escorting role on the sidelines. With the United States fully committed to the defeat of Hitler, there was a distinct feeling among the crews of the escort vessels and those of the merchant ships that, although the road ahead was certain to be hard and stony, the ultimate victory in the Atlantic was certain. It was not only the knowledge of American industrial skills, which could probably be harnessed to produce new ships at least as fast as the U-boats could sink them, that induced this feeling. It was also the belief that together the two great western democracies just had to triumph over the power of Nazi Germany, no matter how great and how painful the cost.

So 1941 ended on a note of hope, even though it had been a difficult year. The U-boats had sunk 2,171,745 tons of merchant shipping, and the Allied and neutral losses from all causes, which included aircraft, mine and raider, had reached the heavy total of 4,328,558 tons. At the end of 1941 Germany had 86 operational U-boats, of which 15, much to Dönitz's disgust, had been ordered into the Mediterranean to assist the campaign there. Moreover, another 35 had been moved on Hitler's orders to the waters west of Gibraltar, some of them destined for the Mediterranean, others to operate against the Sierra Leone convoy route. That left 36 U-boats in the Atlantic to attack the convoy routes, and of these 12 were under orders to concentrate off the U.S. coast where, in the New Year, they were to create havoc. But on the other side of the picture were 150 more U-boats in the Baltic, either running their trials or working up to operational level. It would not be long before they were ready for the Atlantic. The building program had settled down to a steady 25 new U-boats a month, and it was with fair confidence that Dönitz could look forward to 1942.

There was good progress, too, on the British side of the battle. The escort program was well under way, and a new design of corvette, with greater speed and endurance, was beginning to enter the fleet in substantial numbers. Construction of the larger frigates, ordered under the 1940 building program, had gone ahead and they, too, were beginning to enter the fleet, though much more slowly. But other significant developments on the technical side brought added weight to the defense. The normal "pattern" of depth charges fired at a submerged U-boat when detected by sonar was increased from the original five charges to 10, and on occasion to 14. A detonator was being developed to enable the depth charges to be exploded with a shallower setting—particularly valuable in attack from the air—and soon they would be set off at a depth of 25 feet instead of the original 100 feet or deeper. By the end of 1941, in addition, a new antisubmarine weapon was introduced, an ahead-firing multi-spigot mortar which threw a salvo of contact-fuzed charges about 250 yards. This was the

Hedgehog detonations form a pattern ahead of the ship

Hedgehog, and its importance in the battle against the U-boats was that it allowed sonar contact with the target to be held right up to the moments of attack, a considerable improvement on the older method of depth-charge attack from throwers and stern chutes, where contact was lost during the run in and the attack was completed blind.

More important still, though as yet not operational, was the invention by British scientists of the magnetron, by which it became possible to produce very short wavelengths for radar. As the wavelength becomes shorter, the definition and accuracy increase; this scientific breakthrough was to have a great influence on the battle against the U-boats. By the end of the year the magnetron had enabled radar sets with a wavelength of only 1.5 meters to be produced. They were about to be fitted in Coastal Command's antisubmarine aircraft, where they were to prove doubly useful, for they not only increased the accuracy of detection but also did not register on the submarine's radar search receiver of that time.

Another aircraft development of 1941 in the battle against the U-boats was the Leigh Light, a powerful searchlight used in conjunction with airborne radar. These lights were designed for night attacks on U-boats as they were moving to or returning from their patrol areas, for at night a U-boat normally proceeded on the surface when on passage to charge up its batteries. The airborne radar enabled contact with a surfaced submarine to be made at fairly long range, and the contact was held during the run in. A

RDF antenna dominates the bridge of a U-boat

few seconds before the attack, when proximity to the target caused the radar contact to fade away, the Leigh Light was switched on, illuminating the target brilliantly and catching it unawares. Use of the Leigh Light retained the element of surprise for the attacking aircraft. Until it was developed, the plane had needed to drop a flare to light up the target before attacking, giving the U-boat time to dive.

One more aspect of 1941 needs mention. Escorts were beginning to come forward from the builders' yards in fairly satisfying numbers, so that it was possible now to subject their crews to thorough antisubmarine training instead of sending them straight out on operations, as had been necessary when escorts were so few and convoys so many. An initial sea training establishment was opened at Tobermory, on the west coast of Scotland, and all new escorts were sent there for a month as soon as they were commissioned. Commanded by a boisterous retired vice-admiral, Gilbert O. Stephenson, who was serving in the rank of commodore, the crews were put through their paces with a variety of exercises, alarms, drills and inspections which taught them instant reactions to any situations they might meet in a U-boat attack in the oceans. From Tobermory the escorts went for further training in the Clyde (Glasgow), the Mersey (Liverpool) or at Londonderry, the actual escort bases from which they would be operating. There they were formed into groups of about eight ships, and trained together as a group until each ship had submerged its individuality into the group as a whole, able almost automatically to carry out the group commander's methods without the need for signals and commands. Once included in a group, the escort remained with it throughout, and so acquired additional skills as they gained experience of the Atlantic war.

Before we end 1941, it might be interesting to look at one major convoy battle in some detail to see the general pattern of attack and defense which was emerging. SC-42 was a slow homeward convoy of 64 ships loaded with half a million tons of cargo. It left Sydney, Cape Breton Island, on 30 August, escorted by one Canadian destroyer and three corvettes. It was routed far to the north to bring it close to the Iceland base, and it reached Cape Farewell, the southern tip of Greenland, without incident after seven days at sea.

Back in the Admiralty in London an increasing number of U-boat wireless signals were being intercepted, and their directional bearings indicated that the convoy must have been sighted and that a wolf pack was being concentrated for an attack. The escorts were informed that U-boats were in their vicinity, and the convoy was diverted closer to the Greenland coast in an attempt to throw the submarines off the scent. It was of no avail; unfortunately, the ships in the convoy were making a lot of smoke and the U-boat pack had no difficulty in keeping in contact. On the morning of 9 December a ship that had fallen astern of the convoy reported being missed by torpedoes, but a search carried out by the escorts failed to locate

41

the submarine. Just after 9 P.M. the first in the convoy was sunk, and four U-boats were sighted on the surface, some of them operating inside the columns of merchant ships. Although only four were actually sighted, it was certain that more were engaged in the attack. In the next three hours they sank seven merchant ships, one of them a tanker which exploded into a furnace of flame when she was hit. One U-boat was chased by the destroyer up and down the columns of merchant ships, but she escaped unscathed. Later that night two more merchant ships were sunk, and one of the corvettes reported sonar contact with a submerged submarine. All three corvettes joined in the hunt, but there was no time to carry it through to a kill. There were men in the water to be picked up (each had a small red electric light fitted to his lifejacket to show the escorts where he was), and the convoy could not be left unguarded.

During the next day the escort was reduced by one corvette which was detached to tow a damaged tanker to Iceland, and as soon as it became dusk the U-boats attacked again. They sank two more ships, but two more corvettes, ordered by the Admiralty to reinforce the convoy escort, arrived and almost immediately sank *U-501*. Nevertheless, five more ships were sunk that night after their arrival, and there were no more successes against the attackers.

Next day, 11 September, a fresh escort group from Iceland joined the convoy, and that afternoon two of its members sank *U-207*. Then, mercifully, a fog began to form and by nightfall it had completely shrouded the convoy. The U-boats lost touch, and the convoy made the remainder of its voyage home unmolested. A study of the records captured after the war showed that a pack of 17 U-boats had been ordered by Dönitz to concentrate round the convoy after it had first been sighted, and that during the attack on the first night at least eight of them had operated inside the convoy columns.

This was, perhaps, a typical convoy battle of the period, demonstrating the new wolf-pack tactics which Dönitz had introduced. The basic philosophy of the wolf-pack attack was, as has been mentioned, to assemble sufficient U-boats around a convoy to swamp the escorts by sheer numbers, and no attack was allowed until the numbers were there. U-boats on patrol were spread 10 or 12 miles apart in lines across the suspected convoy routes, and a sighting by any of them was immediately reported to Dönitz. His response was to order the U-boat to shadow the convoy, and to signal orders to the other U-boats to close the shadower and form a wolf pack. To assist in the concentration the shadowing U-boat transmitted homing signals on medium frequency. Only when the pack was complete did Dönitz order the attack to begin. With the shadower still in contact to report any changes of the intended victim's course or speed, the rest of the pack proceeded on the surface to a position ahead of the convoy calculated to ensure a meeting just as darkness had fallen. Then they went in, still on the surface, knowing that no sonar could detect them and relying on their tiny silhouette to give them virtual invisibility from the escorts.

At the end of the night attack the process would be repeated. Leaving one U-boat in contact to shadow through the day, the remainder of the pack used their superiority in surface speed again to take up position ahead of the convoy in preparation for the next night's onslaught. And again and again, until at last the battered convoy reached the safety of air escort and the shadowers were forced to submerge and lose contact.

Not every convoy, of course, suffered in this way. In the U-boat Tracking Room in the Admiralty a picture of the German dispositions in the Atlantic was built up from every conceivable source of intelligence and kept permanently up to date. The most important sources of such information were the U-boats themselves, for the very essence of the wolf-pack theory called for a stream of signals back to headquarters. To order his submarines into position for a wolf-pack attack, Dönitz needed to know every last detail of convoy formation, course and speed, weather conditions in the area—in fact, every snippet of information that might influence the success or failure of any attempted attack. Every signal intercepted by the British direction-finding stations—and very rarely indeed was one missed from any part of the world—gave the position of a U-boat to be added or confirmed on the U-boat plot in the Admiralty. Other positions came from aircraft or ship sightings, from calculations of the time of passage of U-boats reported as having left their bases for patrol, from messages sent by clandestine watchers in enemy-occupied ports, from occasional breaks of the enemy code and cipher signals, and from various other sources. With this picture on their plot, the officers in the Admiralty could often route convoys clear of the U-boats throughout their passage, and many of them came through completely unscathed.

In charge of the U-boat Tracking Room was Rodger Winn, a brilliant young lawyer who had been called in for war service and given rank in the Royal Naval Volunteer Reserve. His acute legal mind could marshall all the relevant facts of any situation and formulate the best course of action, and as the war developed he was able to forecast the future movements of the U-boats with an uncanny accuracy. His opposite number in Washington after the entry into the war of the United States was Commander, later Captain, Kenneth A. Knowles. Together these two men made a formidable team whose contribution to the battle was, in the end, decisive.

Of the convoys that were intercepted and attacked, one of the most distressing aspects was the plight of the seamen in the torpedoed ships. Some had time to get away in lifeboats and life rafts. They had a fairly good chance of being rescued, although there were occasions when a lifeboat or raft was found long after the attack, occupied only by men who had died from cold or exhaustion. Others were blown into the water by the force of the explosion, often with shattered limbs or other wounds. Some were able

Crewman battles flames on the tanker *Pennsylvania Sun*

to take to the water as their ship went under, to swim around to find something that floated which could support them until rescue came. But even though the life belts were fitted with red lights, the men could not be saved while counterattacks were under way. If they were pulled from the water during a lull in the fighting, their chances of survival had been lessened further by the tendency of ships when they sink to cover the water in their vicinity with a layer of floating oil, sometimes an inch or more thick. Tankers, always a prime target for the U-boats, normally exploded in a sheet of flame which gave their crews no chance whatever of rescue, and the spreading oil from their tanks sometimes caught fire, burning lifeboats and men struggling in the water. Sometimes it did not ignite, and men in the water were covered with oil, taking it down into their lungs as they gasped for breath. A great many died horribly from this cause. Many others drowned because the oil with which they were covered made them unable to grip a lifeline or a scrambling net alongside a rescuing ship, or loosened their hold on a floating piece of timber. Those working below in boiler and engine rooms when a ship was torpedoed had little chance of getting clear when their ship was hit.

There are no words that can adequately express the courage and devotion of these merchant seamen, sailors of many nations, neutral as well as Allied. Unlike the escorts, they had no means of defending themselves or hitting back at their tormentors; always they were on the receiving end.

Yet, after rescue, they were the first to sign on again when a crew was needed to take a ship to sea, and there were many of them who survived the ordeal twice and three times, and still were ready to return to the fight against the U-boats and the everlasting fight against the sea.

It was, in 1941, an endless story: Britain's desperate need for supplies of every kind to continue the battle against Germany and Italy, matched against the ferocity of the enemy attack by sea and air on the vital supply line. There was no rest for the men in the escort vessels; the delivery of a convoy at its port of destination had to be followed by an immediate return to sea to give protection to another. In the Atlantic it was almost entirely an Anglo-Canadian effort, with the two navies acting as one. It was on the little ships, mostly overage destroyers and corvettes, that the entire burden of escort lay. Perhaps Samuel Eliot Morison, the eminent historian of U.S. naval operations in World War II, has best summed up this phase of the Atlantic battle. "Nevertheless," he wrote, "the story of this Anglo-Canadian period of transatlantic convoys is a glorious one. Thousands of merchant vessels were taken safely across by a distressingly small number of armed escorts, losing less than two per cent . . . For two years, summer and winter, blow high, blow low, destroyers and corvettes slogged back and forth across the North Atlantic, protecting precious cargoes that enabled Britain to survive."

5. Ciphers and Counterattacks

In spite of the feeling of general confidence in Britain at the start of 1942 that, with the United States now a full fighting partner in the alliance, the worst might be over, the year started disastrously in the Atlantic. Although the new corvettes, with improved habitability, fighting power and endurance, were beginning to become operational, and the faster, twin-screw types, later classed as frigates, were well on the way, there was still a chronic shortage of all the varied requirements of a full convoy system. It made itself most manifest in the number of promising U-boat hunts which had to be abandoned prematurely so that the convoys should not be left defenseless. A submerged U-boat located by sonar is very rarely killed or severely damaged by the first pattern of depth charges dropped in its vicinity. Far more often a long period of systematic hunting and attacking is necessary before enough damage is caused to force the submarine to the surface where it becomes a sitting duck. A convoy cannot stop in mid-ocean while its escort group takes two or three hours, and sometimes much longer, to hunt a U-boat to destruction. And so it was that many of Dönitz's submarines, located and attacked, lived to tell the tale and sail again, simply because there were still not enough escorts both to provide protection to the merchant ships and at the same time to take the fight to the U-boats.

With the development of the Iceland air bases it was natural to route the convoys as far to the north in the Atlantic as possible in order to take the maximum advantage of the air cover available from there. The refueling aspect of Iceland was by now not so vital as it had been, for by 1942 many of the new escorts had enough built-in endurance to take a convoy right across the Atlantic without the need to refuel. But against this advantage had to be set the prevalence of winter storms in those waters; both merchantmen and escorts suffered in those tempestuous seas. Frequently, too, convoy voyages were prolonged because the ships had to slow down in the heavy weather, and the crews were worn out physically by the daily battle against the elements. The winter of 1941–42 was a particularly bad one in the northern waters of the Atlantic.

By the beginning of 1942 Admiral Dönitz was well aware that he had fallen far short of the estimated 700,000 tons of shipping a month which he reckoned had to be sunk if Britain was to be brought to her knees. The actual U-boat average in 1941 had been 180,000 tons a month, though Dönitz believed it higher because of the tendency, perhaps understandable, of his captains to overestimate the tonnage of the ships they had sunk and to underestimate the number of ships which, though hit by torpedoes, yet remained on the surface and eventually reached port. Perhaps, in Germany, only he and his U-boat commanders had cause to welcome the entry of the United States into the circle of Germany's enemies, for here was opening up a new opportunity to reach, or at least approach, his monthly target. Two days after the German declaration of war (11 December 1941) Dönitz received permission from the General Staff to wage a U-boat campaign in American coastal waters, an operation to which he gave the somewhat evocative code name of *Paukenschlag*—Beat of the Kettledrums.

But not just yet. Japan had taken Germany by surprise in her action at Pearl Harbor, and the new plans were not fully worked out. And much to Dönitz's disgust, the German naval staff had insisted on a reinforcement of U-boats in the Mediterranean to avert a collapse in North Africa. There were, in December 1941, 12 of the large new 1,100-ton U-boats available, which Dönitz had earmarked for the campaign on the American seaboard. The German naval staff, however, ordered six of these to be sent into the Mediterranean to reinforce the existing U-boats already there. The remaining six sailed for the U.S. east coast at the beginning of January 1942, and they were later reinforced by a further six of the smaller 750-ton U-boats ordered south from the northern convoy routes.

It turned out to be a submariner's paradise. There was no convoy system in force, and hence few problems in attack and little risk of retaliation to the U-boats, and large numbers of merchant ships sailed independently and unprotected along well-defined routes close inshore. A partial convoy system was introduced in April with the help of 10 British corvettes and two dozen antisubmarine trawlers transferred to the United States at the

British tanker goes down off Cape Hatteras, 24 January 1942

end of March. During the next three months a much more integrated and satisfactory convoy system was gradually evolved, and by the end of July it was so successful that the U-boats were withdrawn from U.S. coastal waters to search for easier prey elsewhere. But they had caused havoc during their seven-month stay in American waters, a state of affairs which Morison described as "a merry massacre."

For the first three months of 1942 the U-boats were not allotted definite patrol areas in this theater, but were allowed to roam at will. They found the perfect conditions for sinking ships. All the navigation lights of lighthouses and buoys were still burning, thus removing any problems of navigation, and there was no coastal blackout, so that ships using the main traffic channels off the coast were silhouetted at night against the bright lights burning ashore. During the day the U-boats mostly lay submerged to seaward of the main traffic line, marking down the progress of the merchant ships. As darkness fell they surfaced and closed in for the kill, having easily worked out the probable positions of the ships they had observed by day. In the first six months of 1942, 12 U-boats sank nearly 500 ships in these waters, almost all of them sailing independently, a large number of them oil tankers, almost invariably the most valuable type of merchant ship serving the Allied cause. It was of this period that Admiral Dönitz wrote, in the summer of 1942, "Our submarines are operating close inshore along the coast of the United States of America, so that bathers and sometimes

48

entire coastal cities are witnesses to that drama of war, whose visual climaxes are constituted by the red glorioles of blazing tankers." It was no more than the truth; thousands of pleasure seekers at Virginia Beach on 15 June saw, for example, two large freighters torpedoed before their eyes. It was of these months, too, that the U-boat captains wrote, describing it as their "second happy time."

A new feature of this campaign was the use of what the German Navy called its "milch cows," which were 1,600-ton U-boats converted into U-tankers. Between March and August six of them were sent to sea to sustain the offensive—on one occasion three were operating simultaneously in the area—and by their refueling service they doubled the operational endurance of the smaller 750-ton U-boats.

In the first seven months of 1942, which included the Beat of the Kettledrums operations, the U-boats sank overall a total of 681 ships of 3,556,999 gross tons. The monthly average, therefore, was 508,143 tons, not all that far short of Dönitz's target of 700,000 tons a month. In June, in fact, the U-boat sinkings were 144 ships of 700,235 gross tons, a fraction above the target. If the losses of ships from other causes—air attack, mines, surface raiders—are added, the seven-month total is increased to 4,775,519 tons, giving a monthly average of 682,217 tons.

Losses such as these were perilously close to, if not over, the limit that could be borne by the Allies without falling over the precipice into defeat. They pointed inexorably to the immense importance of the battle against the U-boats in the context of the war as a whole, for of these staggering losses the U-boats alone were responsible for just about three-quarters. There was no war leader on the Allied side, American, British or Canadian, who could fail to appreciate that victory in the Atlantic was the only key to victory in Europe, that the successful ending of the war depended entirely on the ability to move millions of men and tens of millions of tons of weapons and supplies safely across the oceans so that they could be concentrated, when the time came, in the only place from which the assault on Europe could be mounted. It was as simple as that.

That time was not yet, but in the meantime it was every bit as important to maintain the only springboard from which the final assault could be launched. That springboard was Britain, and to keep her fit and fighting required a steady stream of supplies, of raw materials, of weapons, of oil, of food—not just in the future, but now as well. Britain had been, and still was being, attacked massively from the air, her cities shattered and her factories put out of action, and she no longer had the industrial capacity, especially in shipbuilding and repair, to supply all her needs from her own resources. The Atlantic was every bit as important for her survival as it was to the outcome of the war as a whole. Without ships to bring in the supplies needed to keep her in the battle she would go down, and if that happened the map of Europe might as well be rolled up for the next century.

This was a scenario which was, of course, unthinkable, but nevertheless the slaughter of ships in the Atlantic demanded that it be thought about. The convoys still had to cross the oceans no matter what the scale of the slaughter; any reduction of the convoy cycles would be courting danger.

They were desperate months, those of 1942, and made perhaps more desperate still by the knowledge that Germany was now reaping the benefit of her massive U-boat building program. Twenty-five new submarines a month were being added to her operational fleet. The Allies could not yet count on inflicting equivalent losses on the U-boats on that scale. Where in the past war years the number of operational U-boats might have been counted in the fifties, in the future they would have to be counted in the hundreds. And it was quite unrealistic to look to the United States for extra help in the Atlantic. She was already contributing two escort groups based on Reykjavik in Iceland, and for the rest she had her plate full, and overflowing, in the Pacific, where she was sustaining the whole burden of the war. The answer would have to come almost entirely from the British and Canadian sides, by the development of new antisubmarine weapons and a steady build-up of strength in antisubmarine vessels and aircraft. No shortcut to victory was visible on the horizon.

During 1942 the first fruits of the invention of the magnetron, in the form of the 1.5-meter radar, were coming forward fast enough to be fitted to some escort ships and to antisubmarine aircraft. The Germans had not yet tumbled to this invention, and the crude search receivers fitted in the U-boats were unable to register such shortwave radar pulses. For a time the defense had an edge over the attack, and U-boats would discover an escort vessel approaching at full speed or an aircraft diving on them to the attack out of the blue without any previous radar warning. This had never happened to them in the past; their existing search receivers had always told them when a ship or aircraft was in radar contact in plenty of time to dive and get clear. It took the Germans about four months to develop a search receiver which could register the 1.5-meter radar pulses and to fit it in the operational U-boats. The search receiver was known as Metox, and with its introduction the temporary Allied advantage was lost.

About the same time antisubmarine aircraft at last began to receive a weapon which could kill a U-boat. The original antisubmarine bomb had been a sad disappointment, and the naval depth charge, which had replaced it, had too many limitations when dropped from the air. Its minimum depth setting for surface use was 100 feet, meant for attacking submarines already submerged and located by sonar. As submarines attacked from the air were invariably on the surface or just in the act of diving (no aircraft of course could sight a submerged submarine), naval depth charges always exploded too deep to do any damage. By 1942, however, the method of attaining a shallower setting had been worked out. Further, they were now filled with a new explosive named Torpex, and the combination made a really lethal antisubmarine weapon.

By 1942 the only pattern on which the Allies could win the Battle of the Atlantic was clear. Surface escort alone could not do it, because there were always enough submarines in a pack attack to swamp the escort forces; air escort alone could not do it, because there was no way an aircraft could locate a submerged U-boat. But a combination of the two was the answer—the air escort forcing the shadowing U-boats to dive and thus lose contact with the convoy they were attacking, and the surface escort keeping the convoy together and hunting to destruction every submarine located by sonar. The pattern called for large forces in both elements—in the air, to fly a continuous patrol round the convoy at maximum visibility range, which is where the shadowing U-boat would be; on the surface, to hunt and kill and yet retain a margin of escort ships to keep the convoy guarded.

Both methods were impossible in 1942. Shore-based aircraft in Northern Ireland, the Orkneys and Shetlands, Iceland, Newfoundland and the mainland of Canada could cover a fair amount of ocean, but their time on patrol with a convoy passing through their area was relatively short because of their low endurance. There was in existence at the time only one aircraft of long-enough endurance in the air to be really worthwhile in the convoy-

U.S. Coast Guard cutter Hamilton is torpedoed off Iceland

escort business, the American-built Liberator, but the competition for these planes from all theaters of war was severe, and the Atlantic came off badly in their overall allocation. Until early 1943 only one squadron of these invaluable aircraft was operational in the Atlantic, and it took a great deal of political pressure to get even that tiny allocation increased. Liberators could operate as far as 800 miles out in the Atlantic from their base, and were obviously ideal for the purpose of convoy escort. They were backed up in the air by Sunderland flying boats, Wellingtons and American Flying Fortresses, but none of these had the range and endurance of the Liberator, and they were always liable to have to leave a convoy when they were likely to be most needed.

It was much the same story with the escort ships, though in their case it was a problem of numbers rather than of endurance. Already some 200 corvettes had been built and were operational; more were on the stocks. The corvette was by now a much improved antisubmarine vessel over the original Flower class, which had been almost impossible to operate in winter North Atlantic conditions. The larger frigates, too, were coming along, and there were still the generally overage destroyers to add to the

U.S. PBY Catalina patrol planes returning to their Iceland base

total. Yet even with this number of surface escorts, the convoy cover was spread thin. By 1942, the system of convoy was worldwide. Escort now had to be provided in the Arctic for the convoys to Russia, in the Mediterranean for the convoys to Malta and in the Indian Ocean. A breakdown of the numbers in May 1942 shows that of the 200 escort vessels

—10 had been permanently transferred to the U.S. Navy
—47 were working in escort groups at Gibraltar, Freetown, in South Africa, in the Mediterranean, in the Indian Ocean and off the Pacific coast of the United States
—37 were allocated to the escort groups based in Britain for Atlantic convoys
—78 were allocated to the escort groups based in Canada and New-foundland though of these, two groups had been lent to swell the U.S. Navy's coastal escort force and four more were used as escorts for tanker convoys from the Netherlands West Indies in the Caribbean,
—6 were with the Arctic convoys to Russia,
—14 had been transferred to help with the Gibraltar convoys
—8 had been lent to the U.S. Navy for convoy work in the Caribbean.

It is a measure of how hard these escort groups had to work just in order to keep the normal pattern of convoys flowing that they averaged 24 days at sea out of every 30. The six days spent in port were taken up with repairs, refueling and so on, giving the crews very little time for rest and recreation.

There was therefore no real margin yet on which to base the virtually cast-iron pattern of convoy protection that could guarantee to the Allies their ultimate victory in the Atlantic. Three years of war had already produced enough operational experience to demonstrate the guidelines on which this particular battle would be won in the face of Dönitz's wolf-pack tactics. German success depended entirely on the daytime shadowing and reporting of a convoy by one or more U-boats, which had to be on the surface to keep up with it, and on the daytime positioning of the remainder of the pack in the convoy's path for the next night's attack, which again entailed U-boats on the surface since they did not have great enough submerged speed to reach their next night's positions in time. If, therefore, convoys could be given continuous air escort throughout their passage, with the aircraft ranging as much as 20 miles ahead, astern and on either beam of the convoy (20 miles being the maximum visibility distance of a surfaced U-boat), the shadowers would be forced to dive to escape airborne attack and would inevitably lose contact. By this time airborne radar had become a reality, so that there would be few if any undiscovered German submarines even in the worst Atlantic weather.

Efforts throughout 1942 to increase the number of very-long-range aircraft which could operate far enough from their bases to cover the whole of the Atlantic ended in frustration; none were forthcoming. An alternative solution had been discovered almost by accident with the conversion of the German *Hannover* into the MAC ship *Audacity*, mentioned in an earlier chapter. The merchant carrier had been created with the object of operating fighters to drive off the German long-range reconnaissance aircraft which were reporting to the U-boat headquarters the position of Allied convoys, but her fighter aircraft had at the same time sighted and reported a number of surfaced U-boats during the attack on her convoy and forced them to submerge when they realized they had been reported. It was quickly appreciated that in these ships lay the answer to convoy air escort in the Atlantic gaps beyond the reach of shore-based aircraft. Four more MAC ships were ordered, and six auxiliary aircraft carriers were to be built under lend-lease in the United States. But the process was slow. Four had been completed and were operational by the late summer of 1942, but the first call on these four came from the Arctic, where the convoys to North Russia were for much of their passage within easy range of German shore-based bombers, and from the North African landings, a major Anglo-American operation whose importance gave it priority over all else. The Atlantic would still have to wait.

The other side of this cast-iron pattern to defeat Dönitz's submarines lay with the surface escorts. It has been shown above how thinly spread they were in May 1942, but, like the U-boats, they were coming forward now in increasing numbers. The existing escort groups were, in 1942, experienced and efficient, but they were working under a strain that could not be maintained forever without occasional relief. So the first call on new production had to go into the formation of more escort groups, so that the burden could be shared, captains and crews given the chance to rest occasionally and the ships themselves be refitted.

The prime responsibility of the escort group was to its convoy—guarding it, rounding up its stragglers and shepherding it along its way. As mentioned above, this left little time for sinking U-boats unless by chance they offered themselves as lambs for the slaughter. Occasionally some were surprised on the surface in the vicinity of the convoy and sent to the bottom by ramming or gunfire. Others succumbed quickly to depth-charge attack, either being blown to the surface (where they could be quickly destroyed) or breaking up under the force of the explosion. Hunting to destruction was usually far too long a job for a convoy escort—one U-boat during the war was hunted for over 36 hours before she was forced to surface—and it was a heart-rending decision for many an escort captain with a submarine caught in his sonar beam to leave his chance of a kill and return to his primary duty.

Corvettes like HMCS *Battleford* were priceless in 1942

The answer here lay in the formation of a different kind of group, one without definite convoy responsibilities but available to reinforce the escort group of a convoy threatened with attack. The business of assembling a wolf pack to attack a convoy reported by a U-boat invariably called for considerable signaling between the U-boats and their headquarters, and with each signal from sea revealing the position of the submarine through radio direction finding, there was little difficulty in the U-boat Tracking Room in the Admiralty in discovering which convoy was being threatened. The assembling of the wolf pack took some time, usually enough to order a group, had one been available, to join the existing convoy escorts. It was this theory which led, as soon as the production of escort vessels allowed, to the formation of support groups designed exactly for this purpose. With such a reinforcement of the escort group there would always be enough antisubmarine vessels with the convoy to take over the hunts and remain behind until they were brought to success or the U-boat escaped.

In 1942, this was not yet possible because of the dual shortage of very-long-range aircraft or escort carriers, and of escort vessels. The time was certainly coming when both these shortages would be overcome and the victory would be assured. In 1942 it was a question of holding out until the dawn of that golden age when the U-boat could no longer pose any threat to Allied shipping.

Here it is necessary to go back some months in time to investigate the state of what was known as special intelligence—the decrypting of enemy signals—and its effect on the war in the Atlantic. As mentioned earlier, the German B-dienst had made great progress in penetrating the British naval code, and as a result the volume of decrypted transmissions—particularly the daily signal sent out every morning from the Admiralty giving the positions of all convoys and the estimation of U-boat dispositions—increased considerably. On occasions, decrypting took too long for the result to be of immediate use to Dönitz, but the B-dienst was getting steadily better at its job and the flow of information into U-boat headquarters was invaluable. With this daily knowledge of convoy positions and progress, Dönitz could easily station his U-boats along lines of search that virtually guaranteed the sighting of a convoy. Knowing from the same source the size and nature of its escort, the cup was his for the draining.

There had been some similar successes on the British side. The Enigma machine, on which all German signals were enciphered, was capable of a very wide variety of settings, any one of which produced virtually a new cipher. Although the machine was used by the Army and the Luftwaffe, and indeed for diplomatic signals, as well as by the Navy, the security consciousness of the Navy was much above that of all other users, and its particular ciphers were far more difficult to break than the others. The Germans, always methodical, organized their ciphers into groups dealing with particular users and later gave them code names. Thus heavy ships of the Navy, such as battleships and cruisers, when on operational sorties used a cipher with the code name *Neptun*, the warship raiders, such as the pocket battleships, used *Aegir*, and so on. The ciphers used by operational U-boats, and thus of most interest for the Battle of the Atlantic, were, at first, *Hydra*, and later, for U-boats directly under Dönitz's control, *Triton*. U-boats training in the Baltic used *Tetis*, and Mediterranean U-boats used a cipher code-named *Medusa*.

The settings on the Enigma machine, within each of these ciphers, were changed every 24 hours. Hence there was nothing on which the British cryptographers could get to work, as each new day brought virtually a new cipher. The first inkling of success came in February 1941, during a combined operations raid on the Lofoten Islands, when a German armed trawler was engaged and her captain killed before he could complete the destruction of all the secret papers on board. A boarding party discovered a set of spare rotors for the Enigma machine, though the machine itself had been thrown overboard.

This partial success, though it did little to help the cryptographers, led to thoughts that other trawlers might be captured and thus provide the essential break-in to the Enigma ciphers. Position fixes by wireless direction finding had established the fact that German trawlers were sending weather reports from sea between Iceland and Jan Mayen Island. An operation was mounted in May 1941 and the trawler *München* was captured, and although the Enigma machine itself had been destroyed, a list of settings for its cipher was discovered. This was a start, but the cipher used by trawlers would not actually be of great use for the Atlantic battle. Then the very next day, came the decisive break. Out in the Atlantic, Convoy OB-318 was being attacked by U-boats south of Greenland, and in a counterattack *U-110*, commanded by Julius Lemp, who had sunk the *Athenia* on the first day of the war, was damaged and forced to the surface. The skipper ordered the engineer officer to fire the scuttling charges, and he and his crew surrendered. For some reason the charges failed to work properly, and the U-boat remained on the surface long enough to allow a British party to get on board. They managed to patch up the submarine and prevent her from sinking—and they also discovered her Enigma machine intact and undamaged with all its settings, together with a mass of other secret documents. Lemp and his crew had already been hustled below decks on the escort ship to which they had surrendered, so that they would be unaware that *U-110*'s scuttling charges had failed to sink her. Later the submarine sank while under tow to Iceland, but her fate was kept a profound secret throughout the war, and indeed the news was not made public until 1958. As she was not claimed by the British as having been sunk, Dönitz had to accept her loss as caused either by an accident or by stress of weather, and as a result he could feel assured that her cipher machine had gone with her to the bottom.

The fruits of *U-110* were immediate and profound. Captured with the machine were the daily changes of setting up to the end of June, and so the reading of Hydra, the U-boat operational cipher, was current. Moreover, the ability to read Hydra as each signal was transmitted gave the cryptographers a break into some of the other ciphers, particularly Neptun and Medusa. There were some gaps after the end of June, while the cryptographers worked out the new machine settings, but in general they were short-lived, and the cipher continued to be read almost without a break throughout the remainder of 1941.

All had looked set fair for 1942, especially as Hydra had continued to be used into the new year. Then, on 1 February, the Germans introduced the new cipher Triton for the Atlantic U-boats. The change completely defeated the cryptographers, and suddenly the most important and valuable source of intelligence for the Atlantic battle was cut off. It was to remain so through almost the whole of the year, and the situation in the Atlantic became one in which the U-boats were able to enjoy persistent and increasing glances behind the scenes of Allied operations while for the Allies the curtain had dropped across the stage as at the end of an act.

Yet, as in the theater, all was not over through the dropping of a curtain. The six or more months during which Hydra had been read currently had provided a valuable insight into the general U-boat organization and the methods by which this vital campaign was being conducted. And the fact that a leopard was changing his cipher did not mean that he was also about to change his spots. One of the values accruing from the breaking of Hydra was the opportunity given the U-boat Tracking Room to compare

U-boat is blown to the surface by a depth charge

the accuracy of its other sources of intelligence with the real thing as revealed by the cracking of the code. This was particularly valuable in the case of radio direction finding, where it had been possible to compare the positions obtained by wireless interception with the position signaled by the U-boat herself. By this means it was possible to sort out the consistently reliable direction-finding stations from those less so, and thus ensure a greater degree of accuracy in the future. There had been other dividends. The Tracking Room had learned the average daily speed of advance of U-boats from their bases to their patrol areas and hence could differentiate between a U-boat on passage and one operational in her area. It knew, too, how long a U-boat could remain in her area before she was due to start her passage back, and it knew the meaning of the individual types of signal made, such as sighting reports, position reports and weather reports. And, though Triton had replaced Hydra in the Atlantic, the latter was still being used by the Arctic U-boats, by minesweepers and by patrol craft. Tetis, too, was still in use in the Baltic. Both these ciphers were still being decrypted, and frequently the information gained from them had some relevance to the Atlantic U-boats. By no means had everything been lost with the dropping of a curtain.

One side result of the introduction of the new Atlantic cipher was the Allied decision early in 1942 to increase the size of the average Atlantic convoy escort to provide additional protection and also slightly to reduce the average number of ships in each convoy. By mid-1942 an average of only about 850 ships a month were crossing the Atlantic in convoy, the lowest number throughout the war, and the consequent drop of imports into Britain was accepted as the price that had to be paid for the greater safety of the merchant ships. During the first six months of the year, with the Germans concentrating mainly in American coastal waters and the Caribbean in order to reap their rich harvests of unescorted ships, the North Atlantic convoys had sailed relatively unmolested. Only one had been savagely attacked. At the end of February a U-boat had sighted and reported Convoy ON-67 about 600 miles northeast of Cape Race, Newfoundland. A small wolf pack of five U-boats assembled, and during a three-day battle it sank eight ships, of which six were large tankers. But, in the main, the northern convoy routes had remained fairly quiet.

With the ending of the "second happy time," as the American coastal traffic was put into convoy, the U-boats were withdrawn from their killing grounds and redisposed for a new onslaught on the convoys. It was not difficult to anticipate the areas in which they would concentrate. Taking the Atlantic as a whole, there were three vital areas beyond the reach of air cover through which convoys had to pass. On the northern route a gap of about 600 miles loomed between the limiting range of aircraft from Iceland and aircraft from Newfoundland. It was known as the Greenland air gap, and through it had to pass the outward bound ON and ONS convoys, and the homeward bound HX and SC convoys. Down to the southeast were two large gaps beyond the ranges of aircraft operating from Cornwall, Gibraltar and Freetown; the northern was known as the Azores air gap, the southern as the Canaries air gap. Through the Azores gap passed the Gibraltar and Sierra Leone outward convoys (OG and OS) and the big troop convoys to the Middle East (WS), these WS convoys having to carry on through the Canaries gap. The homeward convoys affected were the SL convoys from Sierra Leone, which passed through both gaps, and the HG convoys from Gibraltar, which had the Azores gap to negotiate. It was in these three gaps that the major concentrations of U-boats were expected.

It was indeed there that they went, and the first convoy they threatened was SC-94, a slow convoy which sailed from Sydney, Nova Scotia, on 31 July, with 33 ships in convoy. Its ocean escort was one destroyer and five corvettes, but fog in Newfoundland had prevented aircraft from joining the surface escort and forcing any U-boats in the vicinity to submerge. On 5 August, when SC-94 had reached a position about 450 miles south of Cape Farewell, the first attacks began. One ship of a group of stragglers being rounded up by two of the escorts was sunk; the remaining five were safely shepherded in. On the 6th, U-boats, now reinforced by others directed to the scene by Dönitz, made another attack. The most satisfying feature of this melee was the ramming and sinking of *U-210* by the Canadian destroyer *Assiniboine*. But the latter's bows were so severely crushed in the

59

ramming that she had to return to base, reducing the surface escort to five corvettes. Two more U-boats were damaged in depth-charge attacks and forced to withdraw from the fight, a further reinforcement ordered up by U-boat headquarters taking their place.

Without any air escort to interfere with their movements, the U-boats had little trouble keeping contact with the convoy, though each time they closed in on the merchant ships they were successfully driven off, being forced to dive by the escorts and then attacked when submerged by the new patterns of depth-charging—10 to 14 depth charges instead of the original pattern of five. The main U-boat onslaught came just after midnight of 7–8 August, a favorite attacking time with German captains when they could count on maximum darkness and, perhaps, a lower level of watchfulness among the ships' crews. But the corvettes were all fitted with the new 1.5-meter radar sets. Every surfaced U-boat coming in was picked up by the radars and forced under in self-protection.

The convoy was not yet within range of the Iceland aircraft throughout 8 August, and during that afternoon the U-boats, again reinforced by Dönitz, made another determined attack. Five ships were torpedoed and

Sailors from a stricken U-boat are hauled aboard an escort vessel

sunk, and in the confusion three more crews abandoned their ships in the belief that they had also been torpedoed. When the attack was over, two of these crews returned on board and quickly got their ships back into station in the convoy again but, most unusually, the third crew flatly refused to do so and the ship, though undamaged, had to be abandoned. She became a little later a sitting duck for a U-boat. During the attack, the corvette *Dianthus* sank *U-379*, and another submarine was damaged so severely that it withdrew from the whole operation and returned to France for repair. There were further attacks throughout the remainder of the 8th, but with their radars the escorts were able to detect the U-boats sufficiently far from the convoy that they were forced to fire their torpedoes at extreme range. They all missed. Just before midnight a destroyer from the Iceland group arrived to reinforce the corvettes.

Very early on the following morning, the 9th, the convoy was met by a Liberator, operating at her maximum range of 800 miles from her base in Northern Ireland. A little later U.S. Navy Catalinas from Iceland joined the escort, and though they sighted and attacked a number of surfaced U-boats, they sank none. However, the submarines were forced under too far away from the convoy to be able to do any damage, and the one or two U-boats that did come within range were firmly dealt with by the escorts, now reinforced by a second destroyer. So the 9th passed without loss to the convoy, and the crews of the escorting ships rejoiced that they had kept the enemy at arm's length. But, although of course they did not yet know it, another reinforcement of U-boats had reached the scene and the subsequent attacks were to be heavy enough to swamp the escort.

The U-boats kept in contact with the convoy throughout the night, and during the morning of the 10th, before the first aircraft arrived, they sank four more ships without loss to themselves. Dönitz, scenting a big victory, ordered an all-out attack, and since he had 11 U-boats still in contact there was an obvious possibility of a substantial kill. By now, however, air escort was continuous, and though no submarine was sunk during the numerous attacks, none reached torpedo range of the convoy. The action continued until midnight, and the day's lack of success decided Dönitz to call his U-boats off to search for another target. The convoy reached its British port on the 13th, unmolested during the last three days of its passage, with 22 ships undamaged and 11, of 53,000 tons, sunk. The bag had cost Dönitz two U-boats sunk and four damaged.

This was a typical convoy action of this period of the ocean battle, with losses on both sides more or less balancing themselves on the basis of an exchange rate of one U-boat for four or five merchant ships. It showed up the value of the new antisubmarine weapons, particularly the 1.5-meter radar, which was very shortly going to be replaced by centimetric radar of much greater range and accuracy and to which the Germans would never find the answer, and it demonstrated the worth of continuous air escort. Although this convoy lost 11 ships to the 18 U-boats Dönitz had flung against it, no merchantman was sunk while aircraft were in company.

Not every convoy, of course, could tell the same story. During September, Convoy ON-127, outward bound from Britain, was attacked soon after it passed beyond range of shore-based air cover. It lost seven of its ships and an escorting destroyer to U-boat attack, with three more merchant ships damaged, without inflicting any loss or damage on the attackers. Here again, every loss occurred while the ships had no air cover, and the fact that the U-boats went unscathed was probably because the escort group concerned had not yet been fitted with their radars.

Much the same story was occurring in the Azores air gap, which the U-boat captains called "the black pit." It was the wartime graveyard of many fine ships. A typical convoy experience there was that of SL-118, which sailed for England during August. It lost three ships to submarines while it was crossing the Azores gap, but the first air cover it picked up— a Liberator operating 780 miles from its Cornish base—attacked and damaged a U-boat. The convoy completed its passage with the loss of only one more ship.

An entry in Dönitz's war diary for 21 August 1942 shows that he, too, realized the difficulties which air cover presented to his U-boats. "The number of British aircraft in the eastern Atlantic," he wrote, "has increased and a great variety of them is seen. They are equipped with an excellent location device [the 1.5-meter radar]. U-boat traffic off the north of Scotland and in the Bay of Biscay is gravely endangered . . . by patrolling aircraft. In the Atlantic the enemy's daily reconnaissance forces us to dispose U-boats far out in the middle of the ocean. It is now known that there are also some types of aircraft of particularly long range which are used as convoy escorts. Air escort has been flown over convoys chased by U-boats nearly 800 miles from English bases . . . If development continues at the present rate these problems will lead to irreparable losses, to a decline in successes, and consequently to a decline in the prospects of the U-boat war as a whole."

The first three or four of the long-awaited escort carriers reached the Atlantic in September but, as has been mentioned, they were required for the Arctic and vital convoys mounting Operation Torch, the invasion of French North Africa. About the same time the first support group—antisubmarine ships without convoy safety responsibilities and thus with the time to hunt to destruction—was assembled. But this group, too, was required for the Torch convoys. It was to be 1943 before either of these war winners was to be seen in the Atlantic.

U-boats were the targets of other endeavors as well. In 1941 and 1942 a considerable effort had been made both to destroy them in their bases and to disrupt their construction by bombing, but these attempts had failed to destroy a single U-boat or to hold up the production of new ones.

U.S. Navy patrol bomber version of the Consolidated Liberator

Another air offensive involved patrols across the two main transit areas to the Atlantic, the Shetlands-Faeroes gap for U-boats operating from Norwegian bases and the Bay of Biscay for the French-based boats. Aircraft fitted with the 1.5-meter radar, Leigh Lights and the new shallow-set depth charges destroyed seven U-boats in these areas, by those means relieving the convoys of that number of potential attackers. The introduction of the Metox search receivers in U-boats had, from about mid-1942, reduced the number of killings by this source virtually to zero, but by the end of the year the new 10-centimeter radar was being fitted in antisubmarine aircraft, and in surface escorts as well, and a new era of killing was about to begin. Nevertheless, even with the new radar, the effect of these killings would never be more than marginal in their influence on the main battles around the convoys.

Toward the end of the year a new commander in chief was appointed to the Western Approaches in Britain. Admiral Sir Max Horton took over from Admiral Sir Percy Noble. It was an appointment which gave some promise of an effective offensive against the U-boats in the Atlantic, for Max Horton, to some extent, would fill the position as poacher turned gamekeeper. His early naval career had been spent in command of submarines. His record in World War I had been particularly gallant, and earlier in World War II he had been the admiral in command of the British submarine fleet. He was to inherit, too, the magnificent work of his predeces-

USS *Santee*—one of the
long-awaited escort carriers

sor in building up and training the escort groups. Under Admiral Noble, the skill and morale of the groups had reached a high pitch of excellence. The new antisubmarine frigates, larger, faster and more maneuverable than corvettes, were also beginning to come forward in satisfactory numbers. No one was yet anticipating an easy way ahead, but perhaps there was a faint glimmer of light at the end of the long road.

It had been a desperate year for the Allies, with the U-boats sinking 1,160 ships of 6,266,215 tons. The total loss from all causes had been 1,664 ships of 7,790,691 tons, over a million tons more than the replacement tonnage of new ships built during the year throughout the free world. The figures were bad enough in themselves, but behind this huge loss of ships lay the loss of crews, of men whose lives had been dedicated to the sea. They had been the casualties in a battle largely unseen and unheralded, a long, grim, groping struggle fought out in the ocean wastes. If the losses among the escorts were at times critical in the context of convoy defense, at least they were of men actively engaged in the deadly game of war, men with the weapons and the technical aids to hit back. The crews of the merchant

ships had no such weapons, no such technical aids. During a convoy battle the men below in the merchant ships, in boiler rooms and engine rooms, hearing all around them the explosions of torpedoes and depth charges, never knew if or when a torpedo was coming their way. It needed a special sort of courage to remain at their posts and keep their ships moving through the holocaust that surrounded them. In a big convoy battle this was a scene enacted night after night, but still the ships came through. Perhaps even more remarkable was that, throughout this stage of the war, no merchant ship was ever held back for want of a crew to man her.

An even greater courage, perhaps, was demanded of the sailors who manned the oil tankers. These were the ships bringing the cargoes that Britain had to have to remain in the war, and they were the targets most prized by the U-boats. Few men could expect to come out of a tanker disaster alive, yet, as was the case with other ships, no tanker ever lacked a crew. And when, in the end, victory came in the Atlantic, it was these merchant ship crews, generally unsung and often forgotten, who had made perhaps the greatest contribution of all.

6. The Midnight Sun

The German attack on the Soviet Union on 22 June 1941 opened up a completely new theater of war. There had been little love for the Soviets in the western nations. The notorious nonaggression pact with Germany of August 1939, which had precipitated the war, followed by the callous partition of Poland, had left a distinctly sour taste in western mouths. The subsequent attack on Finland had made that taste worse. Now, however, there was a common enemy to be faced and beaten, and that was a task that hugely overrode any dislikes or ideological differences. In a broadcast on the evening of the German attack, Prime Minister Winston Churchill pledged all possible British assistance to Russia against the common enemy. There were immediate consultations between Britain and the United States. It was agreed that the primary task was to keep Russia in the war. A Soviet surrender would give the German war machine access to vast supplies of oil, iron and copper ores, food and other necessities which the British sea blockade was attempting to deny it.

The first convoy sailed for Archangel on 21 August 1941—seven ships carrying essential stores and the ground staff for Hurricane fighters that were to operate with the Soviet forces. It was a small beginning, but from it grew a regular system of supply of weapons and military supplies carried in fortnightly convoys along the top of the world. It was late in the season, for the northern winter was just around the corner, when the Arctic ice crept daily southwards, forcing the convoys to sail even nearer the German bases in northern Norway, and when the Arctic spray froze as it was tossed into the air, covering the guns of the escort ships and other instruments on decks and bridges in a foot or more of ice.

Beyond the attempts of a few U-boats to interfere with their passages, or an occasional attack by the weak German air forces stationed at Bardufoss and Banak, there was little German reaction to these early convoys. Hitler's "intuition" had foretold a quick success for his 1941 land offensive, with Russia suing for an early peace before winter brought the land campaign to a halt, and in this confident scenario the convoys across the Arctic Ocean were but a pinprick of little importance. Up to the end of March 1942 only one merchant ship had been sunk out of 158 that had sailed, and only one destroyer out of the convoy escorts—both by U-boats. One other merchant ship had been torpedoed but had reached harbor in tow.

Oddly enough, the violent opposition which the later convoys had to face grew out of another of Hitler's intuitions. In the autumn of 1941 he began to worry about the safety of his northern flank, in Norway, and by January 1942 he had convinced himself, though very few others in the German hierarchy, that the Allies, now including the United States, were planning a major landing in northern Norway. He ordered the new battleship *Tirpitz,* sister ship of the unlucky *Bismarck,* north to Trondheim and recalled from Brest the battle cruisers *Scharnhorst* and *Gneisenau* and the heavy cruiser *Prinz Eugen* to reinforce her. Both battle cruisers were seriously damaged by mines during their Channel dash, and the *Prinz Eugen,* which escaped damage in that operation, was torpedoed by the British submarine *Trident* on her passage north and put out of action for nine months. In her place went the pocket battleship *Admiral Scheer.*

To reinforce the surface ships, Hitler ordered the whole of the U-boat fleet to be concentrated in northern Norway. This order, however, produced such a storm of protest from Admiral Dönitz and the naval staff that the Führer was forced to compromise on 20 percent of the fleet of operational boats. Reichsmarschall Hermann Göring, who commanded the Luftwaffe, was another victim of this intuition. There was no love lost between him and the admirals, and he had reveled in their discomfiture as a result of Hitler's intuition. But they got back at Göring by representing to Hitler that a naval concentration in Norwegian waters would be ineffective without a strong air component, and as a result a large number of Göring's torpedo bomber squadrons were ordered north.

And so it happened that, just as the land offensive in Russia was becoming bogged down and the Soviet forces were beginning to get their second wind, a large naval and air force, concentrated primarily for defense against an imagined invasion, found itself admirably placed for a prolonged and heavy attack against the crucially important convoys.

PQ-12 was the first convoy to sail after the German concentration in northern Norway. Consisting of 15 ships and an oiler, from which the escorting destroyers could refuel during the passage, it left Iceland on 1 March. Because the *Tirpitz* was known to be present in Norwegian waters, the British Home Fleet sailed to provide cover against a surface attack. The convoy's close escort was one cruiser, two destroyers and two whalers. Three other whalers which were to have joined the close escort missed the convoy in the heavy weather and proceeded to Russia independently, two of them arriving, the third capsizing in the Barents Sea.

Despite the Admiralty's fears, PQ-12 reached Archangel without loss, apart from some damage caused while steaming through pack ice. On 5 March it had been sighted and shadowed by a German reconnaissance aircraft, whose report brought the *Tirpitz* and three destroyers out on the 6th to make a killing. The *Tirpitz* was sighted by the British submarine *Seawolf* patrolling off the Norwegian coast, but at too great a range to be attacked. She reported the sighting on the evening of the 6th, and the Home Fleet, already at sea as cover for the convoy against just such an eventuality, altered course to intercept the *Tirpitz* and bring her to action. The situation, on the face of it, looked promising.

The day of the 7th was a curious one of hide-and-seek. Visibility varied, down to about a mile during the Arctic squalls, up to 30 miles in the intervals between them. Since the returning convoy from Russia, QP-8, was in these same waters, four groups were in the picture—the two convoys, the *Tirpitz* and her destroyers and the Home Fleet, with the *Tirpitz* searching for the convoys and the Home Fleet searching for the *Tirpitz*. For most of the day the four groups were never more than 100 miles apart, and both the convoys and the *Tirpitz* had narrow escapes from being sighted by their respective adversaries. An unfortunate straggler from QP-8 crossed the path of the German ships and was sunk by gunfire, but she was the day's only victim. No other sightings were made by either side. There were none, also, on the 8th, though the *Tirpitz* again came near. By the end of that day, Admiral Ciliax, commanding the German sortie, had had enough and broke off the search to return home. Although it was no part of the actual convoy operation, a search flown from the aircraft carrier HMS *Victorious* on the morning of the 9th found the battleship off the Norwegian coast. Torpedo bombers from the carrier carried out an unsuccessful attack.

The convoy had got through to Russia unscathed, but the actual operation held profound lessons for both sides. The *Tirpitz* had had a very narrow escape; better trained air crews could have seriously damaged or even sunk her, as the *Bismarck* had been in similar circumstances. The lesson to the Germans was that, without fighter support from the air force, valuable surface ships should not be risked in waters within reach of the British Home Fleet. Since continuous fighter cover from shore-based airfields was

The battleship *Tirpitz* at anchor in a Norwegian fjord

impossible at the distances at which operations against the convoys would take place, it was decided to send out the *Tirpitz* only after reconnaissance aircraft had reported that the British Home Fleet, if at sea, had no aircraft carrier with it. In the meantime, so important was it to cut off the supplies to Russia, the Germans decided to mount the main attack on the convoys with U-boats, aircraft and the remaining surface forces, particularly destroyers, while keeping the *Tirpitz* in reserve—mainly for defense against the Allied invasion that still troubled Hitler's mind.

The lesson to the British was that the Home Fleet would have to sail with each of these convoys. The Admiralty was sure that, after the experience with PQ-12, the Germans were unlikely to risk the *Tirpitz* again except in clearly favorable circumstances. But, obviously, the absence of the Home Fleet as distant cover for the convoys would be a favorable circumstance. It was also appreciated that, without the regular use of the *Tirpitz*, the attack by other means (mainly U-boats and aircraft) would certainly be stepped up to new heights. In the U-boat Tracking Room the build-up of the U-boat fleet in northern waters was noted as a forecast of many bitter battles.

The next four pairs of convoys, PQ-13–16 and QP-9–12, had varied fortunes, though the scale of the attack progressively mounted. With each eastbound convoy to Russia was sailed a westbound convoy to Iceland, mainly of empty ships returning. They were timed to pass each other in the vicinity of Bear Island, the most dangerous area for concentrated attack, so that the distant cover provided by the Home Fleet gave them protection simultaneously. Sometimes the Arctic weather helped the convoys with gales, fogs and patches of Arctic "smoke" which would lie on the surface of the water and shroud the ships even in fine weather. There were other occasions when the weather helped the Germans, for a thin haze could form at a height of 1,000 or 1,500 feet above sea level, providing admirable cover for attacking bombers. The worst enemy, perhaps, was the season of the year, for during the summer months there is no night darkness in those northern latitudes, only at best a perpetual twilight. Worse still were the nights when the aurora borealis was active, for it provided a northern backdrop of brilliant light against which the convoys were vividly silhouetted.

With the exception of one convoy, which was widely scattered in gale-force winds shortly after sailing and found itself in thick drift ice, merchant ship losses were lighter than had been feared, though still very heavy in comparison with the percentage of loss in the Atlantic convoys. Taking these convoys as a whole, around 15 percent of the merchant ships were

Captain of a torpedoed merchantman answers a hail from the enemy submarine

sunk, the majority of them by air attack. The losses among the escorts were heavy, including two cruisers, the *Edinburgh* and the *Trinidad,* a class of ship particularly valuable at that period of the war when there were continual calls for Home Fleet operations. By coincidence the same admiral was flying his flag in each ship as she was sunk; by an even odder coincidence the *Edinburgh*, hit earlier by a torpedo in an action against German destroyers, discovered on clearing the wreckage that the torpedo which did the damage was one that she herself had fired. The intense cold had solidified the oil in the engine and caused it to run in a circle.

Rear-Admiral Bonham-Carter, who survived both these cruiser losses, had no doubts about the dangers of running convoys during the months of the midnight sun. "I am convinced," he wrote, "that until the aerodromes in North Norway are neutralised and there are some hours of darkness, the continuation of these convoys should be stopped. If they must continue for political reasons, very serious and heavy losses must be expected. The force of the German attacks will increase, not diminish. We in the Navy are paid to do this sort of job, but it is beginning to ask too much of the men of the Merchant Navy. We may be able to avoid bombs and torpedoes with our speed, a six or eight knot ship has not this advantage."

Judged purely as an operation of war, the running of these convoys during the summer months was certainly unjustified in view of the scale of losses already suffered, and still to be suffered if they were to be continued. But the political requirements were overriding. It was essential to convince Russia, at that particular time reeling under the 1942 German summer offensive, that her allies in the west were still fighting at her side. Even if the supplies reaching her via the Arctic Ocean were reduced by enemy action to no more than a trickle, that trickle was psychological evidence that the Soviets were not being abandoned to their fate. Come what may, and in spite of all the losses to be endured, the next convoy in the cycle must be sailed.

So began the preparations for Convoy PQ-17. It was suggested that, for ease of maneuver in Arctic waters and when under air attack, a convoy smaller than usual should be sailed, but once again political considerations intervened. American munitions for Russia were piling up in Iceland, and to Russian clamor for them was added American pressure to get them moving. Nevertheless, there were strong feelings in the Home Fleet and in the Admiralty that these operations were hanging perilously on the edge of an abyss, for it seemed certain that the Germans must very soon bring out their heavy ships to supplement the U-boat and air attack, not only to try to convince the Allies that this supply route to Russia was totally uneconomic in terms of modern sea warfare, but also to be able, for home consumption, to announce a victory that would counteract the ever growing cost of the eastern offensive. Moreover, in the last four convoy battles Germany had lost all the destroyers, sunk or damaged, which had been stationed in the north. It was thought in England that these reasons would provoke a determination to send out the big ships on the next possible occasion.

Much the same thoughts were occupying the Germans. The naval command in the north was not happy about the effect on the morale of crews who saw their heavy ships lying idly in harbor while the whole burden of the attack fell on the U-boats and aircraft. The fuel situation, which had been a limiting factor in the case of big ships, had been eased by new deliveries. Even Hitler, whose approval was required before the ships could put to sea, had been persuaded of the necessity, though he hedged his approval with restrictions which made such an operation virtually impossible of success. The signal of approval to operate the big surface ships against the next convoy contained these conditions: "Better short-lived operations with partial success than a prolonged attempt at complete success. Should the situation appear doubtful, do not hesitate to disengage. On no account allow the enemy to score success against the main body of the fleet." It is difficult to imagine instructions more cramping to the commander of an operation; what they said in effect was that once his ships were at sea, their safe return to harbor was more important than inflicting damage on the enemy. By this time four heavy ships were based in northern Norway—the *Tirpitz* and *Hipper* at Trondheim and the *Scheer* and *Lützow* at Narvik. The Germans intended, as soon as the next convoy was sighted at sea, to move the Trondheim ships up the coast to Narvik and the Narvik ships to Altenfjord, close to the North Cape. There, as soon as the Home Fleet had been sighted and conditions were considered safe, the latter ships would be joined by the ships from Trondheim, ready to sail against the convoy at an opportune moment. The actual surface attack on the convoy was to be made in the Barents Sea, east of Bear Island, in waters in which, it was thought, the Home Fleet would be reluctant to operate because of the threat from German aircraft.

The Luftwaffe, elated by its successes so far against the convoys, was practicing a new tactic. The plan was to confuse the antiaircraft fire of the escorts by launching a high-level dive-bombing closely integrated with a torpedo attack from aircraft flying at a height of about 300 feet in a line-abreast formation. The name given to this new plan was the Golden Comb, and 42 torpedo bombers were flown up to the airfields at Bardufoss and Banak to reinforce the existing air concentration. They arrived in early June and spent the next three weeks in perfecting their technique.

So both sides made their plans for what each believed would prove a decisive encounter, though on the British side, in the light of previous experience in these waters, there was no great confidence that the convoy could be fought through without savage losses. A plan formulated in the Home Fleet to reverse the course of the convoy if the German ships sailed within range of the fleet's carrier aircraft was not approved by the Admiralty, which in the case of surface attack preferred to defend the convoy by

Convoy PQ-17 forms off the west coast of Iceland

the Home Fleet while it was west of Bear Island and by submarines when east of that point. For that purpose 18 British and four Soviet submarines occupied patrol areas around the North Cape, in waters through which the German ships would have to sail. A rather more ominous Admiralty note was struck in a telephone conversation with the commander in chief of the Home Fleet, in which the First Sea Lord, Admiral Sir Dudley Pound, said that under certain circumstances he might order the convoy to scatter. This went against the experience so painfully gained in the Atlantic throughout the past three years, which had proved that against air and U-boat attack the best defense was to keep a convoy well closed up for mutual support (most merchant ships now carried two guns, one of them antiaircraft, manned by naval crews). A convoy that had scattered was quite impossible to defend.

PQ-17, consisting of 35 merchant ships, sailed from Iceland on 27 June. One of the merchantmen grounded while leaving harbor, and a second was damaged by drift ice in the Denmark Strait and had to return to harbor. The remaining 33 sailed on with a close escort of six destroyers, four corvettes, two submarines, two antiaircraft ships and three small rescue ships. Additional close cover was provided by a force of four cruisers, two of them American—the *Wichita* and the *Tuscaloosa*. Distant cover was provided by the Home Fleet, which included on this occasion the battleship USS *Washington*.

The convoy was sighted and reported by German U-boats and aircraft on 1 July. Though some attacks developed, they were beaten off with ease. The German surface ships started their preliminary moves on 2 July, but the pocket battleship *Lützow* did not get far; she ran aground as she left harbor. All the others proceeded as intended, though three of the four destroyers screening the Trondheim group also put themselves out of action when they ran aground on arrival. On the following night the *Tirpitz* and the *Hipper* sailed again and joined the *Scheer* in Altenfjord. The departure of all these ships was duly noted in the Admiralty.

Meanwhile the convoy was more than holding its own, having passed to the north of Bear Island during the night of 3–4 July without loss. But early in the morning a single aircraft torpedoed one ship, damaging her to such an extent that the crew had to be taken off by a rescue ship and the damaged merchantman sunk. During the day a few half-hearted attacks, none of them successful, were made by aircraft; then, about 8 P.M., some 25 German aircraft appeared. Three ships were hit, of which two had to be sunk; the third, a Russian tanker, "holed but happy" as the escort commander reported, was able to continue. Three aircraft were shot down and one more was damaged. The convoy was in good heart, well closed up and

Torpedoes strike one of PQ-17's freighters (note barrage balloon, 1.)

elated at having shot down so many of the enemy. Commander Jack Broome, who commanded the escort, wrote in his report, "My impression on seeing the resolution displayed by the convoy and its escort was that, provided the ammunition lasted, PQ-17 could get anywhere." They were by now well over halfway home, with only another 800 miles to go.

Back in London a high-level conference was being held in the Admiralty. Already the close cover of four cruisers, under the command of Rear Admiral L. H. K. Hamilton, was farther east than had originally been intended. The initial plan had been for them to break away to the westward on reaching 25° East, and they were now about 28° East. No more had been learned of the movements of the German ships beyond their arrival at Altenfjord. It was easy enough to calculate that if they had left Altenfjord during the evening of the 4th, they could reach the convoy about 2 A.M. on the 5th. Even if the four cruisers stayed with the convoy, they would be no match for the *Tirpitz,* and both they and the convoy would be annihilated. It was an agonizing decision that had to be made. No one at that conference had any illusions as to the probable fate of the convoy if it was ordered to scatter. The resulting isolated groups would present easy targets to the U-boats and aircraft in the vicinity. At 9 o'clock that evening the decision was taken, and signals were sent ordering the cruisers to retire at high speed and the convoy to scatter.

Three signals were sent. Their wording caused consternation in the convoy. Arriving at about 10-minute intervals, they read: "Most Immediate. Cruiser force withdraw to westward at high speed." Then, "Immediate. Owing to threat from surface ships, convoy is to disperse and proceed to Russian ports." Finally, "Most Immediate. Convoy is to scatter." The cumulative effect of these three signals was electric, giving the impression that the *Tirpitz* and her consorts were just about to appear on the horizon. The cruisers, with their three screening destroyers, turned back and started their ordered withdrawal, and Commander Broome decided to add his six escorting destroyers to the cruiser force for the battle which, he thought, lay immediately ahead.

But in fact, none of the German surface ships had sailed. Hitler was still too apprehensive to let them go, and it was not until noon on the following day, when reconnaissance had established that both the Home Fleet and the cruiser force were too far away to intercept, that he gave his permission. A Soviet submarine fired two torpedoes at the *Tirpitz* but missed; a British submarine reported the sailing of the ships but was too far away to attack. Later that evening, when this report was decoded, the ships were recalled; the German naval staff calculated that with this knowledge the Home Fleet could close the area sufficiently to launch an air attack from its carrier.

The nearest the Germans got to any of the merchant ships was 300 miles, but the ultimate fate of the convoy was almost as bad as if they had

American freighter *Carlton* is a PQ-17 casualty of 5 July

reached it. Once the order to scatter had been obeyed, there was no hope of defense. The remaining escorts tried to pick up small groups of ships and give them some sort of protection, but finding them all was an impossible task. Twelve were sunk on the 5th, six by aircraft, six by U-boats. An aircraft sank another on the 6th, and a U-boat four more on the 7th. Of the entire convoy of 33 ships which had left Iceland, only 11, and some of those damaged, reached Archangel. One of the 11 did not get there until 28 July, nearly three weeks after the first ship in the convoy had arrived.

While PQ-17 was being so heavily mauled, the 35 empty ships of QP-13 were making their way homeward. Much of the convoy's passage had been through thick weather with little visibility, and though it was sighted and reported, no attacks were made on it, the unhappy PQ-17 engaging the full attention of U-boats and aircraft. QP-13 reached Icelandic waters in safety, there to split into two parts, one homeward to Scotland, the other round the north of Iceland to Reykjavik. The ships had sailed through fog for two days and, with no sun or star sights possible, there was considerable doubt as to their position. The Reykjavik group was being led by a minesweeper which had gone ahead to make a landfall. Sighting what she took to be North Cape, she altered course accordingly. But what she thought was land was in fact an iceberg, and a few minutes later she blew up in a British defensive minefield. It was too late to save the merchant ships. Four were sunk and two seriously damaged before the remainder got clear. It proved a sad ending to a previously successful passage.

U-boat pokes through debris from a PQ-17 steamer

Following PQ-17 slaughter, U-boats return to Norwegian base

PQ-17 was the greatest convoy disaster of the war, a tragic mixture of human error and ill fortune. That it occurred so far away on the edge of the ice added a poignant postscript to the disaster, for no survivor, unless picked up in a few minutes, could live in that icy and inhospitable sea. With ships being sunk in ones and twos, separated from their friends, there was very little hope for their crews. And because they could have had no knowledge of the events that had precipitated the sudden disappearance of the escort charged with their safety, many of the seamen must have felt that they were being abandoned just when the danger was greatest, and being left to die alone. And that, perhaps, was the unhappiest aspect of the whole tragedy. It was not true, though the Admiralty's handling of the matter was not universally admired, then or later, but it was difficult to explain in terms that a sailor, engaged in what was recognized as the most hazardous theater of operations, could readily understand and accept.

After the PQ-17 disaster, there was pressure from the Admiralty to suspend the convoy cycle to Russia until the season of perpetual daylight in the Arctic was over. But it was not to be. Once again, as before the sailing of PQ-17, the political necessity of keeping the supplies moving to Russia overrode the naval reluctance to undertake such unremunerative operations. Winston Churchill's motto, so far as the Arctic convoys were concerned, was "In defeat, defiance," and he put forward a proposition to fight the next convoy through using the entire Home Fleet as its close escort. The idea was, perhaps, adequately bold, but in the then-delicate state of balance in the war as a whole it was taking a risk out of all proportion to the possible gain. The Admiralty politely turned the proposition down and proceeded to make less expensive plans for the next convoy.

As things turned out, that convoy had to be delayed until September. Russia was not the only war front clamoring for supplies; in equally desperate straits was Malta, the key to the whole Mediterranean strategy of the war. Before the next convoy could sail for Russia, one had to be fought through to Malta. Ships from the Home Fleet were needed to help do the job.

7. Operation Pedestal

By the middle of 1942 the situation of Malta was becoming desperate. The island had been under heavy air attack for over a year and its population was facing starvation in a virtual state of siege. An attempt had been made in June of that year to run in two convoys to revictual the island and replenish its rapidly dwindling supplies of oil and other war essentials. Two convoys had been sailed simultaneously—one of 11 merchant ships from the eastern end of the Mediterranean, the other of six from the western—in an attempt to confuse and divide the enemy's naval and air forces. Both were failures, even though they had been given escort forces comprising virtually every British warship in the Mediterranean with additional reinforcements from the Home Fleet. Only two of the 17 merchant ships had reached Malta, and the cost to the escorts had been one cruiser and five destroyers sunk, and one cruiser and several destroyers severely damaged.

Malta's situation in the middle of the Mediterranean made it particularly difficult to supply. The island was within a few minutes' flying time of Italian and German airfields in Sicily, and the only possible convoy route from the west was within the same flying time of Sardinian airfields. Italian naval bases at Cagliari (Sardinia) and Palermo and Catania (Sicily), and the motor torpedo boat base on Pantellaria were all close by. The Italian main fleet base at Taranto was near enough to contribute battleships and heavy cruisers to any attack on a convoy, while Italian and German U-boats could lie in wait the whole length of the convoy route. Airfields in Tripolitania could also contribute to the attack.

All this meant that the passage of any convoy to Malta was certain to become a major operation of war, with main fleets engaged in the battle. It was likewise certain to cost a number of ships, since the cards were inevitably heavily stacked in the enemy's hands. By its very nature a convoy of merchant ships moves slowly across the sea, and it is thus a relatively simple target for a warship with three or more times its speed. It is almost equally easy prey for U-boat or aircraft. En route to Malta, a convoy could not be concealed from the enemy, for there was no room to maneuver in the Mediterranean as there was in the Atlantic. And if a convoy escaped all those attacks, an additional hazard awaited it in the waters around Malta itself, which had been strewn with mines.

Nevertheless, by August of 1942 Malta was again approaching its last gasp and another convoy had to be attempted, whatever the cost. The island had been kept going—just—through June and July by heavy reinforcements of fighter aircraft flown from carriers which had sailed eastward from Gibraltar to within range of Malta. These additional fighters had been able to break up most of the daily German and Italian bombing attacks with which the enemy had expected to bring Malta to its knees. A few other bare essentials had been brought in by submarine and by the fast minelayer *Welshman*, whose ability to steam at 45 knots gave her a chance to reach Malta unscathed. But these relatively tiny supplies could not possibly solve the major problem of keeping Malta operational and her population fed. The British government was unfaltering in its determination that Malta should not fall, and the First Sea Lord was equally determined "to accept the inevitably heavy risks in order to achieve a success worthy of the effort." A convoy would be fought through during August, for Malta had reached the state of now or never.

The escort force that was assembled consisted of two battleships, three aircraft carriers, six cruisers, one antiaircraft cruiser and 24 destroyers—a massive escort for any convoy in any waters. In addition, eight submarines were sent out both to patrol areas through which the convoy would pass and to watch the sea routes which main units of the Italian fleet were expected to take if they decided to join the attack. The heavy ships of the escort were to see the convoy safely past Sardinia, but would turn back there, leaving three cruisers, the antiaircraft cruiser, and 12 destroyers to go the rest of the way to Malta. The close escort was then to collect the two merchant ships which had reached Malta during the June convoys and bring them back to Gibraltar. The actual convoy itself consisted of 14 merchant ships. It sailed from the Clyde, on the west coast of Scotland, on 3 August.

Seas wash over the deck of a patrolling German submarine

The convoy passed Gibraltar in dense fog during the early hours of the 10th and thus escaped the watching eyes of the German and Italian agents operating in Spain. But it was discovered on the next day, and enemy aircraft began shadowing it during the morning. The secret of its sailing was out, and the first casualty was suffered in the early afternoon when *U-73* fired four torpedoes into the aircraft carrier *Eagle* and sank her. About the same time the aircraft carrier *Furious*, which was not a part of the escort but was ferrying more Spitfire fighters to Malta, flew them off to complete their journey by air. On her return to Gibraltar one of her destroyer screen rammed and sank the Italian submarine *Dagabur*, a slight consolation for the earlier loss of the *Eagle.*

The enemy air attacks began on the evening of the 11th and continued on the morning of the 12th. They were launched from the Sardinian airfields by squadrons whose standard of training was perhaps less expert than it might have been, and they achieved nothing. They were, in effect, only preliminary sorties; the major air attacks were still to come. As the ships came even closer to Sardinia, the enemy's crack, well-trained squadrons were brought into operation, and the first big attack, consisting of about 80 aircraft, reached the convoy shortly after noon on the 12th. Dive-bombers, fighter bombers and torpedo bombers struck simultaneously, in order to confuse the antiaircraft defense. One merchant ship was so damaged that she could not keep up with the convoy, and later that evening she was destroyed by air attack off the coast of Tunisia.

By now the convoy was sailing through waters patrolled by Italian submarines, which fired a number of torpedoes. All of them were evaded by emergency turns, and one U-boat—the Italian *Cabalto*—was hunted down and forced to the surface by destroyers, where she was rammed and sunk.

So far the convoy had not done badly, but it was now approaching the really dangerous waters, the narrow Skerki Channel between the Tunisian coast and the western end of Sicily. It was also very close to the point where the heavy ships of the escort would have to turn to the westward for their return to Gibraltar. Just before that point was reached, another large air attack came in, this time with more than 100 aircraft engaged. No merchant ship was hit, but the carrier *Indomitable* was damaged by three bomb hits on her flight deck, and a destroyer was hit and so badly crippled that she had to be sunk later. A few minutes later the heavy escort left, and the convoy continued under its protection of cruisers and destroyers. It had not yet won clear of the U-boat–patrolled waters.

The enemy submarines were now concentrated in the Skerki Channel. Two attacks were made about an hour apart, an air raid being thrown in between them for good measure. In the first U-boat attack the antiaircraft cruiser was sunk and another cruiser put out of action. One merchant ship, the tanker *Ohio*, was also hit but was able to continue steaming. With so little sea room in the narrow channel, the convoy was inevitably bunching up a bit, and so presenting an easier target. It was just at this moment that about 20 German aircraft made their attack, unhappily a few minutes after the covering long-range fighters from Malta had left for home. Two of the merchant ships were sunk and another damaged, though not severely. Hardly had the German aircraft departed than another U-boat attacked, inflicting some damage on one of the only two cruisers remaining.

Malta was getting nearer now, and once through the Skerki Channel the convoy closed the Tunisian coast, rounding Cap Bon during the hours of darkness; the hope was that the ships would be less visible against the dark line of the shore. The danger along this stretch of the route lay in the proximity of the torpedo boat base on Pantellaria Island, no more than 40 miles away. These boats were out in force during the night and for about three hours harried the convoy and its escort. The last undamaged cruiser of the escort was hit and fatally crippled early during the attack. Later four merchant ships were sunk and another damaged. This was a particularly sad blow, since the convoy had come so far with such success.

Malta was now within a day's sailing. The convoy's original strength of 14 merchant ships had been reduced to seven, of which two were so damaged that they kept up with difficulty. But it was reaching waters in which a patrol line of six British submarines was operating, and hence was now virtually free from any danger of attack by Italian heavy warships. Reconnaissance aircraft from Malta had reported a movement south of a squadron of four Italian cruisers and eight destroyers on the evening of the 12th, but if they were making for the convoy they were discouraged early on the morning of the 13th when the British submarine *Unbroken*, on patrol north of Sicily, torpedoed two of the cruisers. In fact, no enemy surface ship, apart from the motor torpedo boats based at Pantellaria, ventured south of Sicily.

The remaining dangers for the convoy lay in the air and in the minefields around Malta. Danger soon materialized. Shortly after daylight on the 13th, a new attack by German bombers developed. They hit a merchant ship, which blew up. The tanker *Ohio*, which had already been damaged in an earlier attack, received further wounds when an enemy dive-bomber, which had just released its bomb, crashed onto her deck. But the fires which were started were quickly brought under control, and the tanker struggled on. More air attacks inflicted further damage, one merchant ship being set on fire and two others, of which the *Ohio* again was one, brought to a stop. After rough repairs, they were able to get going again, though at a reduced speed. While destroyers of the escort were sent back to look after the three cripples, the remainder of the convoy, now reduced to three ships—of which one was damaged—fought its way eastward. An hour later it was under the umbrella of Malta-based fighters, which beat off all other attempts to interfere with its progress. Early in the afternoon it made contact with the local escort force of minesweepers and motor launches, and in another two hours it entered the Grand Harbour at Valletta.

There remained the three crippled ships still at sea. Enemy aircraft were making a dead set at them to keep them from getting in, while destroyers and minesweepers were equally determined that they should reach Malta if it were humanly possible. In spite of almost continuous attacks the three kept going until, just as dusk was falling, two of them were hit again. One was sunk; the other, which was the *Ohio*, was brought to a stop. One of the destroyers escorting her was lashed to her side to help her steer a steady course, and two minesweepers took her in tow. There were no air attacks during the night. But progress was painfully slow and Malta was still a long way ahead when dawn broke on the morning of the 14th.

The other crippled ship reached Malta during the morning of the 14th, making four merchant ships safely in harbor. Only the tanker was still at sea. She was, perhaps, the most valuable ship of the entire convoy, since she carried the fuel required for Malta's aircraft. These fighters were of special importance. During the next few weeks they were to attack the shipping which was to sustain the German offensive in North Africa, an operation designed to drive the Allied army out of Egypt. It is a matter of history that the work of the Malta-based aircraft caused this offensive to be postponed because of the lack of seaborne supplies. Yet the *Ohio*, on which it all depended, was still at sea, battered and almost unmanageable, subject to continuous air attack throughout the day, and making no more than about two knots under tow. Somehow all the attacks were beaten off, somehow the *Ohio* remained afloat.

All through that day and the following night she battled on, and on the morning of the 15th the entrance to Grand Harbour was in sight. The great stone ramparts of Valletta were black with people as the *Ohio* was maneuvered through the harbor entrance, and the Grand Harbour echoed with their cheers as the indomitable ship anchored behind the shelter of the breakwater. It was only the splendid courage and determination of her master and crew that had made it all possible. The master of the *Ohio*, Captain D. W. Mason, was awarded the George Cross, the highest decoration for valor which could be given to a noncombatant.

This Malta convoy, typical of the desperate attempts to keep the island supplied, was the last great effort required. The five ships which reached Malta brought 32,000 tons of supplies, and by further small replenishments brought in by submarine and the fast minelayer, the island was kept alive until in October 1942 the Battle of Alamein was fought. The subsequent Allied advance along the North African coast, with its many airfields from which ships at sea could be covered, opened the way to rapid and adequate supply. With the North African coast firmly in Allied hands, there was nothing to stop the merchant ships, and a few months later Malta was able once again to operate as a main naval base and play its full part in the Allied invasions of Sicily and Italy.

It is a measure of the difference in conditions between the Mediterranean and the Atlantic that this convoy, which was code-named Operation Pedestal, was considered a success in the Mediterranean while it would have been a disaster in the Atlantic. The losses had been formidable. Of the 14 merchantmen which originally set sail, nine were sunk and two more so severely damaged that they only reached Malta in a sinking condition. To fight the convoy through had cost the Navy one aircraft carrier, two cruisers and a destroyer sunk, another aircraft carrier and two more cruisers damaged.

The Malta convoys of 1941–42, of which the one described above was fairly typical, are classic examples of the supreme value of convoy as a principle of naval war. Malta had to be held and supplied; it was a strategic base from which submarines and aircraft were able to operate against the seaborne supply lines which alone could maintain General Rommel and his German-Italian army in the North African campaign. If Malta had fallen into enemy hands, the entire Allied strategy in the Middle East would have collapsed, and the way would have been wide open for a junction of German and Japanese forces in the Indian Ocean. The island lay in waters completely dominated by the enemy, and the only way it could be held

Torpedoes claim a tanker victim

and kept supplied was by the passage of merchant convoys fought through regardless of the many risks involved. Operation Pedestal, like the similar Malta operations which had preceded it, accentuated the two vital ingredients of the operation of convoy in the face of an enemy determined to disrupt it. The first was the realization by the escorts that the safety of the convoy was their primary responsibility regardless of any other naval duty, allied to a resolution to get the convoy through. Up in the Arctic, Convoy PQ-17 had failed because the close escort had been drawn away, leaving the convoy unguarded, in the belief that a surface attack was building up over the horizon. In the Mediterranean, Operation Pedestal was successful because the close escort never took its eyes off the merchant ships in its charge. It remained with them through all attacks, holding back the enemy as best it could and going back for the crippled ships to help them through their difficulties.

The other vital ingredient lay with the masters and crews of the merchant ships. Unlike the crews of the escorts they were untrained for war; their work had been performed on the peaceful voyages of their ships across oceans untroubled by unexpected enemies out to sink them. In their cases, wartime convoy called for a very special brand of courage. In the stilted language of his official report, Admiral Syfret, who was in overall command of Operation Pedestal, paid his tribute to them when he wrote that every officer and man of the Royal Navy who saw "the steadfast manner in which the merchant ships pressed on their way to Malta through all attacks will desire to give first place to the conduct, courage and determination of their masters, officers and man."

Given those two vital ingredients, convoy was unbeatable.

8. On the Brink

By the end of 1942 the situation in the Atlantic was beginning to look desperate for the Allies. It was not that Britain was being forced out of the war through the inability to import enough supplies to keep going, though there were acute shortages in many industrial and social areas. It was much more the impossibility of beginning to build up the forces, and their equipment and supplies, needed to carry out the Allied strategy in western Europe.

It was obvious that the war in Europe could not be allowed to stand still and drift into stalemate. It was equally obvious that a major initiative had to be taken somewhere to relieve the intolerable pressure on the Soviet armies. And finally, it was clear that the war could only be won with a major Allied invasion of the Continent. There was no possible alternative.

The key, and the only key, to all these strategic requirements lay in the Atlantic. A clear-cut victory there would open the road to an accelerated and massive build-up of force in preparation for an Allied return to the European mainland. The lack of such a victory would mean that the road would remain barred. The build-up in preparation for the offensive, known as Operation Bolero, had in 1942 fallen far short of even the minimum requirement. This shortfall had contributed to an enforced change in major

British destroyer *Walker,* which did escort duty in the Atlantic and the Arctic

strategy by substituting an invasion of North Africa in place of pressing forward with plans for the more widely desired, and potentially much more decisive, invasion of northwest Europe.

By the end of 1942, Admiral Dönitz had a total fleet of around 350 U-boats, of which about 180 were operational. The remainder were undergoing trials and training. The building program was still in full swing, and it was certain that the number of operational boats would increase each month. In fact, by March 1943 the figure had increased to 235, which meant that, allowing for U-boats on passage to and from their bases, resting and refitting, somewhere around 70 U-boats were actually operational in the Atlantic, having reached their designated areas. In practice there were more than that, for the U-boats on passage—some already allocated to their wolf packs—combed, or raked, the probable convoy routes in the hope of making an attack while on their way outward or homeward. By this means their effective time on patrol was considerably extended. It was even more extended by the growing use of the big U-tankers to refuel the smaller U-boats. By the beginning of 1943 several were in service in the Atlantic.

By this time the entire convoy operation in the Atlantic had been fully integrated with the American coastal convoy system, which meant that the departure point for eastbound Atlantic convoys could be moved to New York. Local escort groups were formed to take the convoys along the coast, being relieved by other groups as they reached the limit of their particular area, until the convoy reached the point where the ocean escort group would take over for the actual Atlantic crossing. Then, having arrived at the other end, local groups there could take over to conduct the ships to their final ports. It was all organized to achieve the greatest economy of time and fuel consumption. As a group delivered its convoy to the next group allotted to it, it would pick up and escort another convoy on its return route. Each convoy now included a tanker fitted for refueling at sea, so that the escort no longer had to break away to a refueling base when it began to run short of oil. Most convoys also had a special rescue ship, whose sole purpose was to pick up the survivors from torpedoed ships. This task had earlier been performed by one of the escorts, but there had been some desperate occasions when survivors had been left to their fate because the escort screen could not be weakened.

New construction of frigates and corvettes, added to an increasing number of destroyers allocated to the escort groups, had enabled the average strength of escort for each convoy to be increased. During 1940 each convoy had had only one or two escorts; in 1942 the average number had grown to five; now in 1943 it averaged seven. This was certainly a considerable improvement, though still inadequate for a convoy sighted and reported by a U-boat and subject to a wolf-pack attack. The normal Atlantic convoy now consisted of 60–65 ships, sailing in columns of three or four ships disposed abeam, the columns 1,000 yards apart and the ships in column 400 yards apart. A 60-ship convoy covered an area of sea of six miles by two miles, and a screen of seven escort ships could never surround it with a continuous sonar watch and could just barely provide a continuous radar watch—provided that the weather conditions were good and that no escort left her position to investigate a contact. Even with seven escorts there were bound to be gaps. A wolf pack of 10 or 20 U-boats, and more often than not a second pack of equal size, would not find it all that difficult to discover the gaps and skip through them.

By early 1943 the new 10-centimeter radar had been fitted in all surface escorts, and the U-boats had no answer to it. When the earlier 1.5-meter radar had been introduced, the Germans had developed their Metox search receiver, which gave a warning of radar contact. But it could not register the centimetric pulses. German scientists had not believed it technically possible to build such a set, and it was not until an RAF bomber fitted with a centimetric set was shot down over the Netherlands in February 1943 that its existence was discovered. The German Navy began work on a new search receiver, but development proceeded slowly and the result was not successful. In any case, the project was at one point held up for some months because a U-boat had reported during March that its Metox receiver, fitted with an improvised device, had given a visible warning of pulses which had not registered on the audible scale (Metox gave an audible warning of the interception of metric pulses). The U-boat command jumped to the conclusion that the answer had been discovered, gave the device the name of Magic Eye, and immediately ordered large-scale production. Disillusionment was slow, and it was three months before the myth of the Magic Eye was exploded and the problem thrown back at the scientists.

The success of the centimetric radar effectively disguised the value of another aid to the detection of U-boats that was now being fitted in the leaders of the escort groups. This was a high-frequency direction-finding (HF/DF) set which was able to take a bearing of a high-frequency radio signal. One of the features of high-frequency signals is that the wave is directed upward and is bounced back to earth by the ionosphere. This feature produces a "skip" distance around the transmitter, so that the signal wave cannot be read within about 100 miles of the ship making the signal. But at the same time the transmitter produces a ground wave which extends to a distance of about 30 miles, and as this wave is direct and not bounced back to earth, it can produce a very accurate bearing when intercepted on a direction finder. During a big convoy engagement with several submarines in contact, the U-boat command's need for detailed and up-to-date information so that it could direct the tactical battle required a considerable number of signals from the U-boats making the attack. As they would all be well within the 30-mile radius of the ground wave, a large number of accurate bearings could be obtained. An escort ship sent steaming out on the bearing was almost certain to find the U-boat and force her to dive, thus at least making her lose contact and at best providing an opportunity for direct attack with gun or depth charges.

Since "huff-duff," as HF/DF was called, proved to be one of the most valuable aids in the protection of convoys, it is surprising that the Germans never suspected that the Allies were using it. U-boat logs of this period of the war have frequent entries recording the sending of signals and the subsequent appearance of an escort ship steaming straight for them at high speed. But the two were never connected. It was assumed that the new British radar was the cause, even though a careful analysis would have revealed that in many cases the first contact must have been made well beyond radar range. This being the assumption, no attempt was made to curtail the signals from U-boats while an attack on a convoy was in progress.

Of the German technical developments, the most important was probably the FAT, a pattern-running torpedo which was hard to elude because it circled among the ships of a convoy rather than running straight. The Germans were also working on the *Zaunkönig*, a torpedo with an acoustic homing device attracted by the sound of a ship's propellers. This torpedo, however, did not make its appearance until midway through 1943. Before that, striking events were to occur in the Battle of the Atlantic.

January 1943 proved no exception to the general rule of storm and tempest during the winter in the North Atlantic, except perhaps that it was more tempestuous than usual. Merchant ships, escort vessels and submarines suffered alike from the weather. It was also not a good month for the U-boats because the British cryptographers had managed to break the Atlantic U-boat's Triton cipher, thus gaining access to information about U-boat concentrations, so that it was again possible to reroute convoys away from them. The U-boat command was, at the same time, getting equally good service from the German B-dienst, which provided Admiral Dönitz with details of convoy positions and courses and often with information about the strength and composition of their escorts. It was probably the very heavy weather, which lasted through most of the month, that prevented the U-boats from making more of this valuable information.

Only one homeward-bound convoy was located and attacked, and here the U-boats sank only one ship. They had better fortune further to the south, where they intercepted and sank 11 independently routed ships or stragglers which had failed to keep up with their convoys, and they scored a considerable victory against a convoy bound from Trinidad to Gibraltar with oil required for the Anglo-American campaign in North Africa. This convoy, consisting of nine tankers, was steaming through the Azores air gap

U.S. destroyer *Roper,* camouflaged for escort work

when it was located by U-boats. It was being escorted by one destroyer and three corvettes, a strong escort for a small convoy of that size, but by one of the mysterious mischances of war their radar sets failed just at the time they were most needed. The convoy was cut to pieces, only two tankers escaping from the holocaust.

All told, German submarines sank during January 37 ships of 203,128 tons, a considerable drop from the monthly average of 1942. Two U-boats were destroyed in the Atlantic during the month, but they were replaced many times over by boats which had completed their trials and training and were ready to join the fleet at sea. A look at the German operational chart for the end of January would have shown 37 U-boats concentrated on the edge of the Greenland air gap, 11 in the area northwest of the Azores for operations against the Gibraltar convoys and 25 disposed south of the Azores and down to the west coast of Africa, lying on the American convoy route to North Africa and across the route of the Sierra Leone convoys. Twenty-seven more U-boats were on passage, giving a total of 100 U-boats at sea in the North and Central Atlantic. It seemed certain that February would be a difficult month.

Merchant ships loading for convoy at a Brooklyn dock

And so it proved. It opened with a savage battle caused by a disturbing, but very rare, event in North Atlantic war history. Early in the month, Convoy HX-224 was attacked by a small pack of U-boats, losing two ships but sinking one submarine in return. A following U-boat, U-632, sank a straggler from this convoy and rescued her sole survivor. Probably in a state of shock following his ordeal, under interrogation he informed his rescuers that a large convoy was following in the track of the one just attacked. This news was signaled to U-boat command, which was able to concentrate two wolf packs in the convoy's path. Contact with this convoy, SC-118, consisting of 63 ships—was made on 4 February. For the next five days a bitter battle was fought between no fewer than 20 U-boats and 10 escort ships, which were reinforced by two American destroyers and supported during the day by long-range aircraft.

This escort, on the face of it, approached the conditions believed by the defense to be necessary for the final victory in the Atlantic. There was, first, a strong surface escort, which amounted to the equivalent of a normal escort group (six or seven escorts), reinforced in the case of an active U-boat threat by a normal support group (another six or seven escorts). This particular surface escort, although its numbers added up to two groups, was not actually made up of two separate groups (one escort and one support), but was one escort group with ships added. The other ingredient was land-based air cover over the convoy. Most of the U-boats engaged in the five-day battle were detected and attacked at one time or another by the escorts; three of them were sunk and two severely damaged. Yet 13 ships in the convoy were sunk, a more than disappointing total in view of the strength of the escort.

The failure of the escorts lay mainly in the lack of integrated training, whereby all the ships forming a group would act virtually as one. This was notably true in the case of the reinforcing destroyers, which had had no group training at all. It was proof that sheer numbers of escorts could never replace the expertise resulting from full and proper training—including not only the actual detection of approaching U-boats and attacks on them, but also such details as signal procedure and communication with escorting aircraft. There were some inadequacies in all these departments in the case of SC-118, including some weapon failures due to human error, which would not have happened with well-trained crews. The battle also demonstrated that, with the short winter day and long night, air cover restricted to the daylight hours was not enough to prevent U-boats from keeping up with the convoy and reaching convenient positions for their night attacks on the surface. Something more was needed, possibly the fitting of Leigh Lights to the long-range air escorts. One final lesson of SC-118 was that, in so long-drawn-out and furious an action, escort ships needed many more depth charges than they could carry. Subsequently, some of the merchant ships carried replenishments, so that escorts would never again be forced to limit the severity of their attacks.

At the time it was thought that this particular convoy was an odd man out, for group training was by now in full swing and tactical schools set up at the main escort bases were developing and teaching the most efficient methods of attack in the various sets of circumstances in which U-boats were liable to be met in battle. Perhaps the training had not been as thorough as it could have been, partly because of the short periods of rest between convoys and partly because the composition of groups had constantly changed, as new escorts were commissioned and old ones went in for refit or damage repair. But under the drive of the new commander in chief, Sir Max Horton, these weaknesses were quickly being eliminated and a new degree of expertise installed in their place. Another new commander in chief, this time of Coastal Command of the Royal Air Force—responsible for air operations over the Atlantic—was also appointed about this time. Air Vice-Marshal Sir John Slessor had much the same driving force as Admiral Horton, as well as a far clearer idea of the true function of air power over the convoys than had his predecessor. So, in spite of the experience of SC-118, there was still a feeling that the upper hand in the Atlantic might be that of the Allies.

The next attacks fell on three consecutive outward-bound convoys— ONS-165, ON-166 and ONS-167. The two ONS convoys were slow, with an average speed of advance of about six to seven knots; the ON convoy was fast with an average speed of perhaps as much as 10 knots. ONS-165, in the charge of an experienced and well-trained escort group whose senior officer was Commander R. Heathcote, was intercepted in the Greenland air gap. Two ships were sunk but the escorts sank two U-boats in revenge, a very satisfactory rate of exchange. As the attacks were made in very wild weather, it is probable that the U-boats were forced to operate at less than their usual efficiency.

The next convoy met a very different fate. The German B-dienst decoded a signal giving its position and course soon after it had sailed, and a strong wolf pack was assembled. For five days and nights the German submarines were in contact, and they harried ON-166 across 1,000 miles of ocean, sinking 14 ships for the loss of only one of their number. Next ONS-167 was attacked, but it got off more lightly. All these attacks were made possible so soon after one another by the milch cows, of which two, *U-460* and *U-462*, were operating in the mid-Atlantic north of the Azores. Between them they refueled no fewer than 27 operational U-boats during this period, enabling the submarines to return to the battle a second time instead of being forced back to their Biscay bases through lack of fuel.

It was clear from these results that there was still a long way to go in the Atlantic. It was also clear from the growing intensity of the attacks—20 or more U-boats were now regularly concentrated against each convoy,

Vice Admiral Royal E. Ingersoll, commander of the U.S. Atlantic Fleet

Admiral King, U.S. Chief of Naval Operations, disliked mixed escort groups

where only a few months earlier half that number would have been regarded as a big attack—that the battle as a whole was reaching its climax. Admiral Dönitz now had the number of operational U-boats he had desired at the start of the war, and more boats were coming forward each month than were being sunk. With this fleet available, Dönitz could afford to throw considerably larger numbers into the attack. The overriding aim was to produce a quick result decisive enough to persuade Britain that her convoy system was a failure. Certainly the system was under great strain at this time. Professor F. A. Lindemann, chief scientific adviser to the Prime Minister, reported, "We are consuming three-quarters of a million tons [of oil] more than we are importing. In two months we could not meet our requirements if this continued." And only a few days later, the monthly Anti-Submarine Report produced in the Admiralty observed, "It appeared possible that we should not be able to continue [to consider] convoy as an effective system of defence." It was as serious as that.

The February 1943 casualty list from U-boats amounted to 63 ships of 359,328 tons; the other causes of loss added another 10 ships of 43,734 tons. Although there had been worse months in the past (807,754 tons in November 1942, for instance), the cumulative effect of the continuing loss of ships was beginning to tell. For these were the figures of total losses; they did not take into account ships damaged by torpedo or air attack which had succeeded in making their way home. Precise damage figures are difficult to establish, but taking an average throughout the war, half a million tons of shipping was under repair every month, and the average time in dockyard hands was six months per ship.

These figures of outright losses and ships under repair need to be set against an annual figure for British shipbuilding of 1 million tons of new construction of merchant shipping. And most of the big building yards were fully occupied with warship building and had little space to spare on their building slips for merchant ships to replace those lost in the war against the U-boats. It was figures such as these that revealed the desperate state of affairs during these bleak months of the war. Some consolation was to be found in the destruction during February of 12 U-boats by sea and air escorts, and another two by air patrols in the Bay of Biscay, but the figures still could not add up to show a credit.

If February had been bad, March was very much worse. It started with a very high-level Atlantic convoy conference in Washington, at which the United States announced its wish to withdraw entirely from its convoy commitments in the North Atlantic. The reason was Admiral Ernest J. King's dislike of escort groups of mixed nationalities, although many such groups with ships manned by Polish, Free French, Canadian, Norwegian and British crews had worked very well in the past. The withdrawal of the U.S. groups already engaged in the North Atlantic was certain to put a considerable additional strain on the Canadian and British escort groups, which were already being overworked, but an agreement was finally reached. The United States would accept greater responsibility for convoy in the South Atlantic and she would contribute one support group to the North Atlantic, under British or Canadian control depending upon whose area of command she was operating in at the time.

Although the importance of this particular support group may not have been appreciated at the time, in fact it proved to be a vital part of the Atlantic campaign at this critical time. It consisted of the escort carrier *Bogue* and five destroyers and was the first escort carrier group to work with the Atlantic convoys. The importance of such a group lay in its ability to close the Atlantic air gap with its own carrier-borne aircraft. Once that air gap had been closed it was theoretically possible to deny to any U-boat a sight of any convoy. The *Bogue* and her support group began operations in March 1943 with the escorting of Convoy SC-123.

March had begun with an attack on Convoy SC-121. Its sailing had been reported to Dönitz by the German cryptographers, and the admiral had concentrated two wolf packs against it, spread in a line of search across her course and right on the edge of the air gap so that the ensuing battle could be fought without his U-boats being harassed from the air. The convoy in fact slipped through the search line without being seen by an enemy submarine, and when Dönitz realized what had happened—a fact again discovered by the German cryptographers—he ordered the U-boats to pursue and catch up. Seventeen did so and were in contact with the convoy for five days and nights from 7 to 11 March. They sank 13 ships without loss to themselves, but there are points to be made in defense of the escort. During the battle the convoy had run into a considerable storm and its ships had been scattered over a wide area. They were in effect stragglers, and no matter how efficient the escort, it is impossible to defend stragglers, particularly against night attack, when every ship of the escort group must be closed up round the convoy itself. SC-121's loss of 13 ships was perhaps a disaster, but with stragglers providing the majority of the individual ships lost, it could not be taken as any indication that the convoy system itself was at fault. It was certainly depressing that no U-boats had been sunk during the long battle. Had there been a more experienced escort group in charge (it was a mixed U.S., British and Canadian group only recently formed), the attackers might have suffered some casualties.

The next convoy encounter showed what could happen when a well-trained and experienced escort group was in charge, though here again there were some disappointments. Convoy HX-228 was being conducted across the Atlantic by Escort Group B3, of which the senior officer was Commander A. A. Tait, a very efficient group leader who had welded British, Polish and Free French crews into a well-trained group. Once again the B-dienst deciphered a signal enabling the Germans to deduce the convoy's present course and speed. Dönitz was able to move up a wolf pack

USS Bogue—the first escort carrier to work with an Atlantic convoy

of 13 U-boats, which he reinforced with five more which had been on passage to their patrol areas to the west. British decrypts of German signals revealed that the convoy was threatened, and a support group was sent to strengthen the defense. This consisted of the escort carrier *Bogue* and her destroyers, of which only two were available at the time. The group joined the convoy on 5 March and remained with it until the 14th.

The first contact was made by *U-336* on 10 March, but its sighting signal was intercepted by HF/DF and it was driven off. *U-444* then came along as contact keeper and was able to home in several more U-boats. Attacks that night sank four ships, one of which had dropped behind the convoy as a result of a previous torpedo hit. One submarine was severely damaged in the violent explosion of a munitions ship that she had torpedoed.

During the attack, HMS *Harvester*, Commander Tait's ship, sighted *U-444*, forced it to dive, then blew it to the surface with depth charges and sank it by ramming. One of the *Harvester*'s propeller shafts got caught up in the U-boat and was badly damaged, and shortly after she got clear her other shaft fractured, leaving her motionless in the water. She was sighted later by *U-432* and sent to the bottom with a torpedo. Almost at once the Free French corvette *Aconit* found *U-432* with her sonar, forced her to the surface with a depth-charge attack and sank her by gunfire. U-boat contact with the convoy was regained at noon on the 11th, but the shadowers were driven off. Long-range attacks by two submarines during the night of the

11th failed to hit any further ships, and on the morning of the 12th the last shadower was forced to submerge and lose contact. The convoy completed its voyage unmolested, having lost four merchant ships and one escort destroyer at the cost of two U-boats sunk and one substantially damaged.

The disappointment in this particular action was the lack of success of the support group, and particularly of the carrier. To operate her aircraft a carrier would need to leave the convoy in order to maneuver freely in relation to the wind direction (aircraft had to fly off and land on with the carrier head to wind), but with only two destroyers of her group to screen her and numerous U-boats on hand, it was considered too big a risk to a valuable ship for her to operate independently.

Possibly another reason for this decision was a big change made by the Germans in the settings of the Enigma machine. A fourth coding rotor was introduced at this time. British cryptanalysts knew of the forthcoming change—it had been foreshadowed in an earlier signal which had been deciphered—and the key word ordering the change was sent out to all U-boats at sea on 8 March. For a time information about U-boat movements and intentions was lost. An Anti-Submarine Division report to the First Sea Lord, dated 9 March 1943, said, "The expected has happened. The Director of Naval Intelligence announced yesterday that information on U-boat movements is unlikely to be forthcoming for some time —perhaps even months."

There followed the biggest and most savage convoy battle of the war, fought for the most part with the Atlantic in its most tempestuous mood. Two homeward convoys had sailed within three days of each other, the slow SC-122 leaving New York on 5 March and the fast HX-229 on 8 March. The sailing telegram of the slow convoy was quickly decoded in Germany, but the equivalent signal for the HX convoy gave more trouble and was not fully decoded for some days. Nevertheless, for the sinking of ships one convoy was as good as another, so far as the Germans were concerned, and Dönitz was able to bring together a massive concentration of U-boats in the path of SC-122—no fewer than four wolf packs, with a total of 44 submarines.

Stormy weather in the North Atlantic held back some of the U-boats, and SC-122 passed unsighted through a gap in the search line caused by the delay. But coming up more or less in her wake was the faster HX-229, and on 16 March this convoy was sighted fortuitously by *U-563*, which in fact was withdrawing from the operation with engine trouble. In the belief that this must be SC-122, Dönitz called down the wolf packs which had been stationed about 100 miles to the northward on the supposed course of the convoy. Their route down to HX-229 should have kept them just clear of SC-122, but as luck would have it, *U-338* caught a glimpse of the convoy and reported it.

HX-229 had been savagely attacked through the night of the 16–17

March and had lost many ships. The convoy escort group, like most of the others in the Atlantic at that time, was below strength because so many escorts were out of action as the result of damage from the wild storms of January and February. With only four ships operational in the group, it was impossible to avoid wide gaps in the defense through which U-boats could make their way. In addition, the rough seas provided poor conditions for both radar and sonar detection. So many submarines were attacking one after another that the defense was swamped. There was no time to investigate every HF signal and every contact, or to stand by all the torpedoed ships and pick their crews up from the sea. All that could be done was to try to throw the U-boats off the scent by emergency turns away from where they were thought to be and to try with brief attacks to force them to submerge after every sighting or contact. A prolonged attack could not be made on even the most promising of contacts, for with the convoy in such danger every available escort had to remain close.

By now the sailing telegram of HX-229 had been decoded in Berlin, but Dönitz still believed that he was dealing with only one convoy. It was not, in fact, until the morning of the 18th that the admiral was convinced that two separate convoys were involved. But now he redistributed his attackers, with 18 U-boats allocated to HX-229 and 13 to SC-122. Twelve had been forced to break off the attack, mainly because of lack of fuel, though two more which had refueled from a U-tanker were called in by Dönitz. A few of the U-boats in the original packs, held up by the storms, had never managed to catch the convoys, but there were enough in contact to threaten heavy losses. By now it was blowing a full gale, with frequent heavy snow squalls over a tempestuous sea and the visibility at times down to nil. Both convoys had lost much of their compact formation in the wild weather, and with the fast convoy catching up the slow they had almost become one vast convoy scattered over a great area of sea.

The huge volume of U-boat signals was evidence enough in the Admiralty U-boat Tracking Room that a big battle was being fought out in the Atlantic, and the direction-finding stations indicated without any doubt which convoys were being engaged. At the time 12 other convoys were at sea, and consideration was given to detaching some of their escorts to assist. But with so many U-boats in the Atlantic in addition to those round HX-229 and SC-122, the risk of weakening the other escort groups could not be taken. All that was available were three destroyers, two American and one British, in Iceland. They were ordered to reinforce the hard-pressed escorts of the the two convoys but were all delayed by the storms. There was to be little relief for the embattled escorts and the laboring merchant ships, facing yet another night of systematic attack. The worse the weather, the less reliable the radar and sonar, those two crutches on which the escorts relied to detect their attackers.

On 18 March every available very-long-range aircraft—nine all told—

Ice coats the U.S. destroyer *Trippe*, on North Atlantic patrol

was sent out to provide air cover. The convoys were just within range. None of the VLRs succeeded, however, as the constant snow showers blotted out their vision and the wireless homing signals sent by the escorts were too distorted to give a reliable bearing. Throughout the day of the 18th and the night of the 18th–19th the U-boats, submerged by day and on the surface by night, continued the onslaught. But at long last the end of the ordeal was in sight. Early in the morning of the 19th both convoys were within 600 miles of home and just coming under the protection of shore-based antisubmarine aircraft based in Northern Ireland. During the day of the 19th the U-boats still in contact tried desperately to get ahead of the convoys in readiness for one more night attack, but they were unable to make headway in face of the air cover. At dawn on the 20th, Dönitz, accepting the inevitable, called the operation off.

Analyzing the reports of his captains and examining all the distress signals from ships in the two convoys, Dönitz calculated that 32 merchant ships of 187,560 tons and one destroyer had been sunk, and torpedo hits on nine other ships obtained. In fact 21 ships of 141,000 tons had been sunk; none of the escorts had been hit. *U-384*, which had been one of the attackers, was sunk during the morning of 20 March, after the operation had been broken off. She was caught on the surface by an air escort a long way—210 miles—from the convoy and failed to dive in time to escape destruction by depth charges dropped alongside her by the aircraft.

One small episode of the attack on HX-229 demonstrated the particular danger to ships which broke convoy. On the evening of the 18th the officers and crew of the 8,800-ton freighter *Matthew Luckenbach* decided, as a result of the incessant attacks on the convoy, that she would be safer out on her own, using her maximum speed of 13 knots. She steamed away, refusing to obey the order of the escort commander to return to her station. Twelve hours later she was hull down on the horizon when she was torpedoed by *U-527*. Although the ship did not sink, her crew abandoned her. By good fortune the column of water thrown up by the explosion was seen through binoculars by an officer in one of the escorts, and help was soon on the way. The crew refused to return to the damaged ship to try to get her moving again, and she had to be abandoned, a signal being sent for a tug to tow her in. Six hours later another U-boat came across her, still floating upright, and sent her to the bottom with a torpedo. It was a needless loss of a good ship.

To Admiral Dönitz this operation was proof of the soundness of his tactics in the Atlantic battle and of his training of new crews in the Baltic, for half the successes here had come from crews who were out on operations for the first time. Hence he could look to the future with confidence. His operational fleet was increasing rapidly; he could now reckon on being able to keep a minimum of 120 U-boats always at sea. Moreover, he was getting invaluable assistance through the brilliant successes of the B-dienst. No longer was it necessary to search blindly for convoys to attack. Fortunately for the Allies, Dönitz still considered the centimetric radar carried in aircraft and escorts to be the most dangerous of the detection weapons arrayed against his U-boats. He completely failed to appreciate the value of the HF/DF receivers, which betrayed the bearing of every U-boat when it sent a wireless signal. Accordingly, he made no attempt to limit signaling when contact with a convoy was made, and the escorts continued to profit from the prodigious talkativeness of the U-boats.

To the Allies, the picture presented by this convoy battle was bleak. Not only had the sinkings been very heavy—12 ships from HX-229 and nine from SC-122—there had been no compensatory sinking of U-boats, apart from the one destroyed after the battle was over. This was perhaps the bitterest pill of the whole operation. It called into question the efficiency of Allied antisubmarine weapons and of the training of the escort crews. Overall, the losses during March were more than disquieting. They pointed to a swing in the campaign which, if continued, could only lead to disaster. In the first 10 days of the month 41 ships of 230,000 tons had been sunk; in the second 10 days the figures were 44 ships of 282,000 tons. What was even more depressing was that of these losses it was not stragglers but the convoys themselves which had provided the major part. And all this was within two months of the Casablanca conference, at which the President of the United States, the Prime Minister of Great Britain and the

Combined Chiefs of Staff had agreed that victory in the Atlantic must be the basic precondition of any future major operation in Europe. Without victory in the Atlantic there could be no victory in Europe.

It was quite certain that sinkings of merchant ships on this scale could not be accepted. If they continued, the whole system of convoy, on which the entire Allied maritime strategy relied, must fall to the ground. Yet there was no alternative system of large-scale supply visible to any naval eye. It was difficult at that moment, in the face of such sudden destruction of essential shipping, to take the longer view and continue to plan ahead on the basis that, whatever lay in store in the Atlantic, it was the convoy system alone that could turn the final trick.

Admiral Horton, on whose shoulders lay most of the burden of the Atlantic campaign, had been pressing hard for the formation of new support groups, preferably based on the small escort carriers. These ships had been coming forward from American yards since 1942 but had been allocated to more essential duties in the Arctic and to the convoys for Operation Torch. Now there were three escort carriers around which groups could be formed. If he could get these operational, Horton counted on killing two birds with one stone, the first by closing the Atlantic air gap with carrier-borne aircraft and the second by having independent groups available to reinforce the escort groups of convoys threatened by wolf packs. The basic requirement here was for extra destroyers with long endurance, in order to screen the carriers when they were operating, but so far there had been none of these invaluable small ships available. Now at last there seemed to be an opportunity of finding them. With the Soviets having survived a second summer campaign by the German armies and with an overland supply route to Russia having been opened up through Iran, the regular convoys to Murmansk could be suspended through the summer months of perpetual daylight. The political need of such hazardous operations was no longer urgent, and their suspension would free about 15 Home Fleet destroyers trained in antisubmarine measures. With these, the carrier support groups would have their essential screens.

Between March and May five new support groups were added to the Atlantic antisubmarine armory, though only two were based on an escort carrier. One of the three carriers available, HMS *Dasher,* was destroyed by an internal petrol explosion before her group could be formed, but even with her loss the air gap could be closed with the other two.

The March calamity also led to a reappraisal of the allocation of VLR aircraft. Coastal Command of the Royal Air Force and the Royal Canadian Air Force, which between them were responsible for providing air cover for the convoys, had been bottom of the list of allocations of these very desirable aircraft, the American-built Liberators. In February 1943 there were only 18 Liberators in the whole of Coastal Command and none in the RCAF, even though trained crews were ready for them. It took President

Roosevelt's direct intervention to knock some sense into all those authorities whose initial clamor had led to a prodigal supply of this invaluable machine, and as a result no fewer than 255 were earmarked for the Atlantic—75 from the U.S. Army Air Forces, 60 from the U.S. Navy and 120 from the British allocation, mainly Bomber Command. They could not all arrive at once, of course, and when they did they needed modification for the antisubmarine role, but at least they were on the way, and with their arrival no convoy in the Atlantic need be without air cover throughout its passage.

It is a matter of history now how close the Allies came to defeat in the Atlantic during the first three months of 1943. If that had happened, it would undoubtedly be a valid argument that the true cause was the lack of VLR aircraft. An addition of only two squadrons at that time would have been enough to prevent the loss of many ships and to save a great many lives.

It was still, to some extent, almost as much a battle between the scientists as between the U-boats and the escorts. The main effort in Germany was directed toward an entirely new type of submarine capable of very

Casablanca conference: Atlantic victory is assigned top priority

high underwater speed. This was the Walter U-boat, in its way the forerunner of the modern nuclear submarine. It used turbines driven by gases produced from diesel fuel, with hydrogen peroxide as the catalyst. There would be no need to come to the surface periodically to recharge batteries, a time when a submarine is always vulnerable. This, together with a very high underwater speed, would have presented an almost impossible problem to the escort vessels of that period. Fortunately for the Allies, the Walter boat ran into many delays and design problems; in fact, it never became operational during the war. But many other scientific improvements were made, including the ability of the new U-boat to dive to depths of 600 feet and over. A new design of torpedo, the Zaunkönig acoustic torpedo, was on the point of introduction, and the magnetic detonator, which exploded a warhead underneath a ship where it did most damage, was greatly improved.

On the Allied side advancements were made in sonar equipment—particularly the "A attachment," which enabled contact to be kept with a deeply submerged U-boat. And a new type of sonar, by which the depth of a submarine could be calculated, was just around the corner. The ahead-throwing Hedgehog, which suffered from the need to obtain a direct hit on a U-boat's hull to achieve a kill, was being developed into a much more lethal ahead-throwing weapon, the Squid, which discharged salvos of three depth charges. The charges themselves were given an additional setting for use against U-boats at great depth and were adapted to reach those depths more quickly after being released. A homing depth charge, or torpedo, was developed for use by aircraft. Radio sonobuoys, which relayed the noise of a U-boat's propellers, were also added to the growing list of technical aids to the destruction of U-boats.

It is easy to list and describe all the technical aids, produced on both sides, designed to bring victory in this essential battle. It is less easy to remember, and to appreciate, that the actual battle itself was between men. It is true enough that they were aided by every technical device and instrument that science could put into their hands, but ultimately it was on the skill and endurance of the men engaged, and on the strength and purpose of their moral determination, that the outcome of the battle depended. There were many times in this Battle of the Atlantic, the longest and most savage battle in the whole history of war, when the advantage swayed from one side to the other, when with those who served in high places on shore on both sides there were periods of gloom and talk of defeat. But there was no such talk among the men actually fighting at sea. The writer can remember visiting U-boat bases in Germany immediately after the end of the war and being surprised at the high state of the morale and discipline of the surviving U-boat crews. Equally he can remember talking with men of the escort ships during the black days when it looked as though defeat might well be just around the corner, and being fortified by

Lieutenant Commander Wolfgang Lüth—a leading U-boat ace

their unswerving knowledge that they were going to win in the end, whatever might happen in the meantime. Writing of the dark period at the height of the Battle of the Atlantic, Commander D. A. Rayner, who led an escort group, presents this picture:

Consider for a moment the men in those ships . . . The U-boats were sinking as many as sixty ships in a single month, as many as there were in one whole convoy—all lost. Yet there was no lcak of men to man the ships. No British ship ever stayed in harbour because she could not find a crew. Was there ever a finer testimonial to our nation?

The bravest ship I ever met was one whom we christened Sinbad the Sailor. We met him first on a homeward bound convoy. He was immediately noticeable, and would have stood out in any company. From what junk heap of worn-out ships had he been rescued to fight in the most terrible of all wars? Almost everything about him went straight up—straight bow, tall slender masts, a very tall and extremely thin funnel. Only his counter was as fine and delicate as a steam yacht. When we first met him smoke was pouring from his slim funnel. We had tried commands, arguments, cajoling—all to no purpose. Sinbad was smoking his pipe. Very soon he was falling out of bed repeatedly [unable to keep up with the convoy]. We put him back time after time. He was so good-humoured about it all that we could not be really cross with him. His captain would come to the rail and wave to me as I called to him over the loud hailer. He was as old as the ship herself. He would stand, a short stocky figure wearing a bowler hat, swaying on the bridge of his ship. The wind fluttered his white muttonchop whiskers, and his red face was always split in a grin of welcome. One imagined he was the owner as well as the captain of his crazy charge.

But one day he could not get back to the convoy. Some defect in his aged machinery had reduced his speed to walking pace. I stayed with him as long as I could. At last, as dark was coming, I received a signal from [the escort commander]: *Leave your straggler and resume your station.* I knew why —there were six U-boats shadowing the convoy.

I went very close alongside.

"Can you not get her going any faster?"

"Nay, Mister—", the words came slowly. I could just hear them above the whistle of the wind and the roar of waters between the ships. "Nay-we-be-launched-over-fifty-years-ago. It's-an-engineer-shop-I-beneeding."

"I am sorry I must leave you—very sorry. We expect attack on the convoy. Goodnight and good luck."

"Ay-you-get-off-to-the-convoy-Mister. We'll-be-all-right-you'll-see."

108

If ever I prayed for anything it was that the U-boats would not find our Sinbad that night. Next morning he was out of sight astern. There had been no S.O.S. in the night, and we had kept a special wireless watch for him . . .

To go to sea in such a crate was to play with death. Yet he went—and had found a crew to go with him. No men could have been braver . . .

9. Turning Point

April 1943 was approached by the Allies with great apprehension after the crippling Atlantic losses of March. There was little argument against the belief that a repetition of the March experience would amount to a clear-cut signal that the campaign in the Atlantic had been lost—that the passage of ships across the oceans in convoys protected by escort groups was no answer to the modern tactics of submarine attack. To those in the know, the continuing failure to break the current U-boat cipher was a further source of concern, as it removed the possibility of rerouting convoys away from concentrations of U-boats. The authorities on both sides of the Atlantic were acting in the dark, now blind where a month or two earlier they had been able to see. All the evidence pointed toward a climax in the Atlantic struggle, a climax from which one side or the other would have to go down to defeat.

The belief that April and possibly May would be the "make or break" months in the Atlantic was also held by the U-boat command in Germany. Postwar study of the voluminous U-boat records, which were captured intact in May 1945 when the war in Europe came to an end, show the depths of that belief and the measures being taken to swing the balance firmly down on the side of Germany. Daily reports of progress in the building yards and on the training schedules of new crews in the Baltic reveal Dönitz's anxiety to swell even further the massive submarine force which he was already deploying in the Atlantic. His frequent prodding of wolf packs to go in and make a great killing during April show his eagerness to equal, if not exceed, the amount of tonnage sunk in March. Both he and the captains of the U-boats had by now the scent of victory in their nostrils.

The pattern for April could be said to have been set by Convoy HX-231, which left New York with 49 ships, of which one was bound for Halifax only, on 25 March. It was a "fast" convoy, with an average speed of advance of nine knots, and was escorted up the coast to Nova Scotia by a local Canadian escort force of two corvettes and a minesweeper. As there were no U-boats plotted in that area the escort, though weak, was adequate. During this passage, four ships broke down with mechanical trouble, one of them a tanker fitted for refueling the escorts in mid-Atlantic, but all four made their way back to harbor without trouble.

Four days later the convoy was augmented by 13 ships from Halifax and four ships from St. John's, all brought out by escorts, so that the total number of ships now numbered 61. The extreme cold, a thick fog and

U.S. Navy blimp keeps watch over an Atlantic convoy

In April 1943 Rear Admiral Francis S. Low took charge of U.S. antisubmarine efforts

patches of sea ice made it difficult to arrange the convoy in its ocean formation of 14 columns of ships, but the formation was achieved eventually, and the ocean escort—B7 Escort Group, led by Commander Peter Gretton in the frigate *Tay*—took over responsibility from the local groups. Gretton's force consisted of six ships—one destroyer, one frigate and four corvettes. They were all fitted with 9-centimeter radar and sonar, but only the frigate had a high-frequency direction-finding set. Although the winter weather still prevailed in the Atlantic, the convoy was given a northerly route to bring it within range of air cover from Iceland after it had traversed the Greenland air gap. Bad weather in Canada had made it impossible to provide air cover from any bases there. No rescue ship was attached to the convoy, since none was available at the time. This lack was to have tragic results.

Meanwhile, from the submarines available in the area, Dönitz had formed a wolf pack of 15, which he named *Löwenherz* (Lionheart). These were spread at 20-mile intervals on a line of search across the expected track of Convoy HX-231. They began near the eastern end of the Greenland air gap and moved westward on the surface at slow speed. Dönitz knew where the convoy was from the information given him by his cryptographers. During the morning of 4 April the fifth U-boat in the line (*U-530*) sighted the convoy and made her report. The admiral repeated the position to all U-boats and instructed *U-530* to keep in contact but not to attack until the others reached the convoy. He also ordered six more U-boats within range to join the Löwenherz group if they had enough fuel to get there. In all, 20 U-boats finally made contact with the convoy, and of these 17 would be involved in attacks over the next four days. Another long signal from Dönitz urged all the captains to attack with the utmost determination at the earliest possible opportunity. Germany, he said, expected a great victory.

Sighting signals sent by *U-530* and by other U-boats as they came up were heard on the frigate's DF set. Escorts were ordered out along the bearings to force the signaling submarines to dive and, with luck, lose sight of the convoy they were about to attack. Three U-boats were sighted and one of them attacked, but, as was often the case, the escort did not have enough time to hunt her to destruction before it had to return to the convoy. This U-boat was *U-594*; she was damaged during an early attack, but not seriously enough to force her to break off the operation. Meanwhile, the various sighting signals had, of course, been intercepted by the shore DF stations, and the positions obtained from plotting their bearings were certain evidence that a U-boat wolf pack was gathering round HX-231; an attack was undoubtedly imminent. This was the typical situation that called for the help of an uncommitted support group to swell the defense, and in fact the 4th Support Group, which had just refueled in Iceland, had already been ordered to join the convoy on the expectation of just such an attack.

The group sailed on 3 April, but with the North Atlantic in a stormy mood the four destroyers took three days to get there.

By nightfall 11 U-boats were in actual contact with the convoy or approaching it. Attacks were made or threatened throughout the night, but only two ships were torpedoed, of which one remained afloat and able to keep her position in the convoy. No submarine was sunk, but two were so damaged by depth-charge attacks that they had to break off the operation and return to base for repairs. More encouraging was the number of U-boat attacks which were driven off before they could develop, in every case by the appearance of an escort which forced the U-boat to dive while it was on the way in. This was one result of the thorough group training introduced by Admiral Horton at the end of 1942. The coherence of the group acting as an integrated whole had proved its worth.

It was during this night that the absence of a rescue ship was most bitterly felt. The merchantman that had been sunk had gone down very quickly. Only one lifeboat and one raft could be launched before she went under. The remainder of her crew took to the water, the red lights on their lifejackets dotting the water, but in the bitter cold of the North Atlantic they had little chance of survival. The frigate *Tay*, after investigating a radar contact, steamed close to the lifeboat on her return to the convoy, but as the group leader she was needed urgently to direct the battle. She could not stop; all she could do was to shout encouragement to the men in the lifeboat and promise to send another escort back to pick them up during the first lull in the battle. This was done, but the corvette entrusted with the duty could find no trace of the boat.

The raft and the lifeboat between them had held 57 men; the remaining 11 men of the crew in the water quickly perished in the cold. By the next morning only five men on the raft were still alive. They joined 33 men in the lifeboat. For the next seven days the seamen drifted in the Atlantic, in weather so cold that a film of ice covered the bilgewater in the boat and their clothes were rigid with frost. Finally they were sighted by an aircraft from Iceland, and later that day a destroyer made a lee while a rescue ship picked them up. Of the original 38 men in the lifeboat, only seven were still alive, and of these, four had to have their legs amputated as the result of frostbite. Such were some of the perils of the Battle of the Atlantic.

But to return to the convoy. Daylight revealed that three ships had broken clear of the convoy, the actual appearance of U-boats making an attack apparently persuading their captains and crews that they would be safer out on their own, away from the target on which the U-boats would undoubtedly concentrate their utmost attention. It was always stressed in every convoy conference, held before sailing and attended by the captain of every participating ship, that to leave the convoy while on passage was virtually to commit suicide. But under actual attack, with ships being torpedoed in the immediate vicinity, the temptation to cut loose and run was obviously very great. In this particular case, one of the three ships had second thoughts and returned to her position in the convoy. She reached her port of destination safely. The other two, one Dutch and one Swedish, continued on their independent way and both were sunk by U-boats with heavy loss of life.

Although the weather continued bad, a certain amount of air cover was available during daylight on 5 April. No doubt it had a considerable effect in deterring attacks. There were still several U-boats around the convoy, and they would unquestionably have attacked it if they had been left on their own. The combination of aircraft watching the perimeter of visual distance of the convoy and the surface escorts zigzagging close to it was enough to instill in most of the U-boat captains a healthy respect for the defensive powers of the escort. Only one daylight attack was made. A lucky shot hit a tanker but did not sink it. There was, however, one further casualty when a straggler, which had fallen astern with engine trouble, was sunk with the loss of all hands. Four U-boats were required to finish her off, and one does not like to dwell on the thoughts of her crew as they endured attack after attack in the wide solitude of the Atlantic.

Liberators bomb and strafe a U-boat (note bullet splashes)

The night of 5-6 April saw the German submarines as determined as ever to attack the convoy and to surface escorts equally determined to drive them off before they could get close enough to fire their torpedoes. In this determination they were unwittingly aided by the U-boats themselves, because every U-boat, as it went in to attack, had orders to make a signal to headquarters. This was thought necessary in order to avoid the danger of collision if two U-boats attacked simultaneously. The first U-boat to signal received the order to go ahead; those which signaled later were told to wait. Thus, the direction of the coming attack was made known to the escort fitted with HF/DF, and the other escorts were warned to look out in that direction.

In all, 17 attacks were made during the night, but each one was beaten off before any damage was done. One U-boat, *U-635*, was sunk. The only ship lost was the merchantman which had been torpedoed and damaged on the first night but had managed to keep up the convoy speed. As the weather worsened during the night her bulkheads began to buckle, and she had to stop her engines and drop astern. There her crew abandoned her and she sank an hour later. Most of her crew were quickly rescued by one of the escorts and an American ship which had gone to her rescue. Only 19 men out of a total crew of 132 were lost.

The day of 6 April saw the convoy well within flying range of Iceland and also of the air bases in Northern Ireland. Air cover was almost continuous throughout daylight hours. During the morning the four destroyers of the support group that had sailed from Iceland also joined, so that HX-231 was now strongly guarded. Sixteen U-boats were still operating against the convoy, but they had little chance of getting through so strong a screen. There was disappointment back in U-boat headquarters at the lack of success of the previous night's attack, and Admiral Dönitz sent a querulous signal to his captains. He urged them not to waste so much time and effort on the stragglers but to concentrate on the convoy with all the energy and tenacity at their command. It is not known what the recipients thought of this signal, but throughout the day and the following night no attacks on the convoy succeeded. On the other hand, aircraft made several attacks on U-boats sighted on the surface, most of them shadowing at extreme visibility range. These strikes succeeded in sinking *U-632* and damaging two others severely enough to force them back to base for repairs.

The convoy itself had spent a quiet day, with no indication that any U-boats were in the actual vicinity, and there were hopes that the almost continuous air cover had kept the U-boats submerged so long that they had lost contact. In fact, however, eight of them were still round the convoy, having kept in touch with it by hydrophone fixes while submerged. But again, no attacks developed, and early next morning, with the convoy south of Rockall Island and on the home stretch, Dönitz called off the operation. Twenty U-boats had succeeded in sinking three ships out of the convoy and

116

Survivor of a sunken submarine yells for help

three stragglers; the Germans had lost two U-boats sunk and several damaged, three of them seriously.

After the disappointing March figures, this convoy was considered to have done well. It did not escape notice that all the sinkings of ships in convoy had occurred before the support group arrived, or that there were no serious attacks after the convoy had reached the area of continuous air cover. These facts bore out the conditions set by Admiral Horton for the ultimate defeat of the U-boats, and although no one expected that one swallow could make a summer, there was still a good deal of satisfaction at the outcome. There seemed, too, to be a certain reluctance on the part of the U-boat captains to commit their boats to the attack, particularly after the surface escort had been strengthened by the support group. Many of the old hands at the game, the aces of the early days, were gone, either killed or languishing in prisoner-of-war camps, and it looked as though the new captains were lacking some of the old dash. This was not, perhaps, surprising in view of the new generation of weapons and detection devices arrayed against them, particularly radar, which they feared because it did not register on their search receivers, and HF/DF, which they so mysteriously ignored. This remained one of the most inexplicable features of this period of the U-boat war, for the German authorities had several photographs of British escort vessels, taken with long-distance lenses from Spain while they lay in Gibraltar, which clearly showed the HF/DF aerial array.

Commander James A. Hirshfield, skipper of the USCGC *Campbell*, an escort
workhorse

HX-231 may perhaps be looked on as the first sign of a swing in the
Atlantic balance. It was not a victory, nor was it a defeat on the scale of
Convoys HX-229/SC-122, described in Chapter 8. An exchange rate of six
ships (including stragglers) lost for two U-boats sunk was at least bearable
in terms of Allied shipping, for the curve of new production of merchant
ships, mainly through the drive of the remarkable Henry Kaiser with his
Liberty ships, was beginning to rise very steeply indeed. It was not yet
quite keeping pace with losses, but there was little doubt that, saving
another calamity on the March scale, it would do so within the next couple
of months or so and accelerate into a healthy surplus.

Succeeding convoys did, in fact, do better than HX-231 on the basis of
ships lost per U-boat sunk. Support groups, particularly those based on an
escort carrier, were making it more and more difficult for U-boats to penetrate the defensive screen around the convoys, and unless they succeeded
in doing that they could never reach an attacking position. Gradually, too,
the very-long-range Liberators were reaching the Atlantic in increasing
numbers, extending the range of shore-based air cover. And perhaps even
more important, British cryptographers had managed to break into the new
Enigma Triton cipher introduced so suddenly at the beginning of March.
More often than not there were delays, sometimes of three or more days,
in deciphering the U-boat signals, but at least there was not the total
blindness of earlier weeks. In the seven successive convoys, homewards

and outwards, which followed HX-231, the exchange rate was approximately one merchant ship for one U-boat.

It was figures such as these that, in the first week in May, prompted a staff report in the Admiralty that ran:

> Historians of this war are likely to single out the months of April and May 1943 as the critical period during which strength began to ebb away from the German U-boat offensive—not because of lower figures of shipping or higher numbers of U-boats sunk, but because for the first time U-boats failed to press home their attacks on convoys when favourably situated to do so.

> The number of U-boats operating was as great at the end of April as it ever has been; U-boat construction still overtops casualties, and despite the increasing effort of our air and surface attacks the U-boat fleet continues to grow in numbers, though more slowly than before. Yet its effective strength appears to be waning.

These words were written during the course of a particularly bitter, and particularly significant, convoy battle which was being fought in the Greenland air gap. A slow convoy, ONS-5, had left Liverpool on 21 April, with the empty ships only lightly ballasted. It was being escorted across by Peter Gretton's group, which had brought over HX-231. It fairly soon ran into rough weather which freshened into a full gale, making it very difficult for the light merchant ships to keep their stations in formation. Nevertheless, all went reasonably well, and on the 26th one of the covering aircraft sank *U-710*, which was lying on the surface ahead of the convoy. This gave rise to the hope that the sinking might have punched a hole in a U-boat patrol line through which ONS-5 could pass undetected. Perhaps this was so, for it was not until two days later that the convoy was sighted and reported by *U-650*. Dönitz had 14 U-boats in the area, and he formed them into a wolf pack with orders to make a night assault on the convoy.

All attacks that night were successfully driven off by the escorts, two U-boats being damaged, but in a daylight submerged attack *U-258* succeeded in getting through the screen and sinking one ship. This, however, was the only success, for the weather was getting too bad even for the submarines to operate. Gradually they all lost contact, the severity of the gale forcing them to submerge, and on 2 May Dönitz called the pack off.

That evening the Third Support Group joined to strengthen the escort, but the convoy had been so badly scattered by the gale that it covered a wide expanse of ocean. Gradually most of the ships were gathered in. Eventually they formed one large and one small convoy about four miles apart, with the small convoy, escorted by a corvette, doing its best to join up with the other.

ONS-5 was now in dangerous waters, particularly with the weather so bad that no aircraft could take off to provide cover. Dönitz had a large group of 30 U-boats (the *Fink* [Finch] wolf pack) spread in a line of search to intercept a homeward-bound convoy (SC-128) of which his cryptographers had given him both position and course. As it happened, SC-128 passed through the line without being sighted, but ONS-5 hit it right in the middle. It was sighted and reported, and Dönitz promptly called up another 11 U-boats that were within range. As the admiral himself recorded in his War Diary, "The initial positions for a convoy battle had never been more favorable. Thirty U-boats of Group *Fink* were in the patrol line, with only eight miles between each [pair], and the convoy was sighted right in the middle of this line. Moreover, eleven boats of Group *Amsel* were ahead of the convoy." The battle was on, and with no aircraft able to fly it would be a straight fight between the surface escorts and the largest concentration of U-boats ever massed against a convoy.

The weather was still bad on 4 May, enough to cause some scattering of the convoy but not enough to make the U-boats break off their attacks. Six ships were sunk during the night and another five during the following day, all for the loss of one U-boat.

Reading the German reports of this battle after the war, one can sense Admiral Dönitz's belief that the tide was turning again and that he had in his hands a victory comparable to those achieved during the March operations. Reports coming in from the U-boats showed that he still had plenty of them close enough to the convoy to mount an attack that would swamp the escorts. He sent them a signal encouraging them to go in again at all costs. Even if they were beset by aircraft, they were not to dive but were to fight back on the surface with their new antiaircraft guns.

Fifteen U-boats went in to the attack that night but luck was against them, a fortuitous fog shrouding the merchant ships from their sight. Bad luck for the U-boats, though, was good luck for the escorts, for fog is no bar to radar. Of the 25 U-boat attacks that night, all were driven off before torpedoes could be fired. Four U-boats were sunk, and no ship in the convoy was hit. Next morning a second support group arrived from St. John's to relieve the one which was with the convoy. As it was approaching, it sank *U-438*. To add to the score, a Canadian Catalina flying boat patrolling near the convoy sank *U-630*.

What had loomed at one time as a possible massacre had in the end turned out to be a considerable victory. Twelve ships had been sunk out of the convoy, but they had cost their attackers eight U-boats. Although it was not known at the time, two more U-boats had collided during the bad weather of 3 May, and both now lay at the bottom of the ocean. In addition, five U-boats reported severe damage and another 12 damage of a lesser degree. These were losses on a scale which no navy could contemplate with equanimity, even though they had occurred in a battle that had run against all previous experience. Perhaps in the hope that this battle was truly an exception, a sort of odd man out, Dönitz decided to continue keeping his biggest concentration of U-boats in those distant waters. The next convoy battles would surely reverse the experience of ONS-5.

The succeeding two homeward-bound convoys—HX-237, of 46 ships, and SC-129, of 26 ships—were both sighted and attacked. Between them they lost five ships, of which three were stragglers, and of the 36 U-boats brought in to attack them, four were sunk. HX-238 got through without being sighted by U-boats. These were results from which it was difficult to predict any decisive swing one way or the other, disappointing for the U-boat command, perhaps, and encouraging for the Allies, but not yet enough to be able to say with certainty that the battle had been won by one side and lost by the other.

The convoys which followed, HX-239 and SC-130, clinched the argument. HX-239 had the British 4th Support Group, built round the escort carrier *Archer*, to supplement its surface escort group and could therefore count on continuous air cover throughout its passage. Although a wolf pack of 14 U-boats was in contact, no ship was sunk and one U-boat was destroyed by an aircraft from the *Archer*. SC-130, however, was probably the convoy which drove the final nail into the German coffin. It was escorted

Freighter pitches in an Atlantic storm

by the group which had brought over Convoy ONS-5, by now a hardened and experienced group, finely trained and led by Gretton. It, too, was strengthened by a support group diverted to it for the three days of battle. Four groups of U-boats were brought into position to attack the convoy, though only 19 succeeded in making contact. Again Dönitz urged his men on. At a moment during the battle when contact with the convoy had been temporarily lost, he signaled, "The convoy absolutely must be found again. Do your best. Success must come tonight."

Both air and surface escorts were at times heavily engaged in beating off the attacks, and they were so successful that not a single ship was lost. But in the wake of the convoy no fewer than six U-boats lay destroyed on the bottom, U-209 and U-381 sunk by surface escorts and U-273, U-696, U-954 and U-258 by shore-based aircraft. Dönitz could not understand it. "We can see no explanation for the failure," he wrote in the War Diary, and he ordered the two most senior and experienced captains engaged in the operations to report to him exactly what had happened.

If Admiral Dönitz had still had any doubts, the results of the operations against these two convoys unquestionably settled them. On 24th May he wrote in the War Diary:

> In the last few days circumstances have arisen which give a particularly strong indication of the present crisis in the U-boat war. These circumstances are :
>
> a. The confirmation of further heavy losses.
> b. The complete failure of the operation against SC-130 as well as the conditions encountered during the attack on Convoy HX-239.
>
> We have to accept the heavy losses, provided the amount of enemy shipping sunk is proportionate. In May, however, the ratio was one U-boat to 10,000 gross tonnage of enemy shipping, whereas a short time ago it was one U-boat to 100,000 gross tonnage of enemy shipping. The U-boat losses of May 1943 therefore reached unbearable heights . . . The enemy air force therefore played a decisive part in causing such heavy losses. This can be attributed to the increased use of land-based aircraft and aircraft carriers combined with the advantages of radar location. . . . To a very great extent the enemy aircraft brought about the failure of our U-boats against Convoys SC-130 and HX-239. In the former they prevented the U-boats from maneuvering into an attacking position ahead of the convoy, so that only a temporary contact could be maintained. In the case of HX-239, the enemy aircraft precluded all contact.

With the benefit of hindsight it is generally thought today that the actual turning point in the Battle of the Atlantic came with the passage of Convoy ONS-5, particularly the operations of the final night of the attack. Following their successes of the previous 24 hours—six ships sunk in the night, five in the day—the captains of the U-boats were at their most ferocious. Possibly stimulated by their admiral's exhortations to provide Ger-

The U.S. Coast Guard cutter *Campbell* camouflaged for action

many with a complete victory, they went into their attacks with all the determination they could muster. Yet all the attacks failed, beaten back by the surface escorts which, moreover, sank four of the attackers. If surface escorts could do this without any help from the air, what was the result likely to be in future operations against convoys when air cover was plentiful? That some such thought began to occupy the minds of many commanders of U-boats seemed to be apparent in a fairly widespread reluctance to get close enough to succeeding convoys to fire at them.

Other evidence suggested that general morale among the U-boat crews was getting shaky. Their general spirit was markedly lower than it had been. With the breaking of the new U-boat cipher in April, many of the enemy's private thoughts and fears were again revealed. Rumors of new Allied weapons were spreading among the crews, most of them quite imaginary. One story was that the surface escorts were using delayed action depth charges suspended on buoys, which would explode after the escort had steamed away. This rumor came to the ears of the U-boat command and generated a signal that such a device "was pure bluff, and it should be realized that bangs do not mean danger. The man who allows his healthy warrior and fighting instincts to be humbugged ceases to have any powers of resistance to present-day enemy defenses." The need for signals such as these was itself more than just a straw in the wind.

All the U-boat captains blamed the new centimetric radar and the increase in air cover for their lack of success. They were of course quite correct, but, again, no one in Germany seemed yet to appreciate the part HF/DF played in the surface escorts, particularly in regard to the operation of aircraft cover. Every sighting and shadowing signal, every signal announcing that a U-boat was going in to make an attack, produced a bearing on the transmitter, and it was a simple matter to order one of the aircraft above the convoy to investigate along that bearing. It got there much faster than could a ship of the escort group, and if it failed to get a kill with its depth charges, at least it forced the U-boat to submerge and lose its attacking position. Looking back from today, it seems surprising that no one in Germany realized that the sending of a radio signal and the almost automatic subsequent appearance of an aircraft or an escort ship meant that some new form of detection was being employed, particularly since in almost every case the aircraft or ship concerned was outside radar range when it began its run.

The most important elements in this sudden change in the Atlantic were the new skills of captains and crews of both ships and aircraft and the mystiques (if that be the word) of operational research. Admiral Horton, commander in chief in the Western Approaches, had neither time nor patience for anything but the best in his officers and men, ashore or afloat. His recipe for the best was continual and hard training, theoretical as well as practical. In addition to tactical schools ashore, where every element of battle against U-boats was studied and the best tactical responses to attack worked out, realistic exercises at sea, using a surface ship to represent a convoy and British submarines as U-boats, accustomed the crews of escort ships as nearly as possible to what they could expect out in the Atlantic. With the new construction of frigates and corvettes coming forward in a steady stream, Horton could now afford the time to train the new escort groups to a very high pitch of efficiency before committing them to the real thing. In the light of the results of April and May in the Atlantic, it was obvious that the new policy of thorough initial training had begun to pay substantial dividends, and that the drive and personal interest of the new commander in chief had produced a new and intense dedication to the job in the crews of the escort ships.

It was the same story in the air. The new commander in chief of Coastal Command, Air Vice-Marshal Sir John Slessor, had very much the same ideas and drive as his naval colleague. He was, perhaps, the first air commander to realize that a U-boat alone in the ocean without a ship to sink was wasting its time, and that to earn its keep it had to come to the convoys. The corollary of this was that the most profitable killing area for U-boats was around the convoys, and it was there that he should concentrate his aircraft. This was a complete reversal of the previous air doctrine in the Atlantic, which had put emphasis on wide searches of the ocean in the hope of pouncing upon an unwary U-boat. Allied to Slessor's new doctrine was a degree of training similar to that imposed by Horton. The growing skill of the aircrews could be measured by the number of U-boats they were now sending to the bottom. It was, by May 1943, almost exactly equal to the number dispatched by the surface escorts.

The work of operational research, continuous throughout the whole campaign, was equally important in achieving the final victory. It was carried out by scientists who worked alongside the men actually engaged in the battle and not in the back rooms with which scientists are habitually associated. The field of research was as wide as the Atlantic battle itself, ranging from the development of new weapons and detection devices to such everyday matters as the most economical size of a convoy in relation to the number of its escorts. The investigators proved, in fact, that the larger the convoy, the more economical the use of escort ships. The proof of this particular pudding came with the eating, and by 1944 convoys of more than 120 ships were being safely escorted across the Atlantic by an escort force only marginally more numerous than that required by a convoy of 40 ships.

It was a similar story with aircraft, where operational research helped to produce startling results. One involved so simple a matter as the color

U-boat is bombed by aircraft from the escort carrier *Bogue*

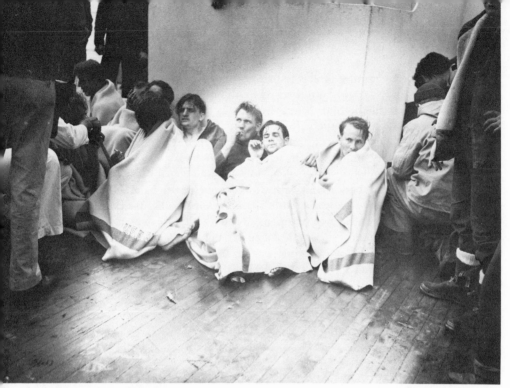
U-boat survivors

the aircraft were painted. It had puzzled the scientists in 1942, when so many U-boats were operating in the Atlantic, that few of them were being sighted by the many aircraft on patrol. It was suspected that because the aircraft were all painted black, they stood out against a normal cloud background and could be seen by a submarine long before they themselves could see their target. At the suggestion of the scientists, they were painted white, and almost immediately the number of sightings was doubled. It was in small ways like this, as much as in big areas such as weapons development, that operational research made a great contribution to the ultimate victory.

The change from the depression caused by the ship losses of March to the elation of the April and May results was too quick and sudden for the Allies to recognize at once that the crisis in the Atlantic had been met and overcome. Obviously they were well aware that things were now going very well where a few weeks ago they had been going very badly. How close Britain had come to physical and industrial starvation, how slender was the margin, had been known only to a few. There had been no wide recognition, even in the Navy—which was most intimately concerned— that the general food and supply situation was desperate. It was nearly touch and go at the end of 1942; starvation and defeat were approaching even more rapidly after the holocaust of March 1943. The general feeling by the middle of May was that the Allies had won a breathing space. It was only later that the magnitude of the change became apparent. There was still a feeling that although the tide of battle had swung remarkably in the past two months, there was still time for it to swing back again.

Yet it had been a victory, even though only a few were yet able to recognize its enormity. The figures tell the story. Taking the six weeks between 6 April and 19 May, 912 ships had sailed in convoys across the Atlantic; 24 of 120,750 tons had been lost—23 to U-boats, one to a marine casualty through collision—and 27 U-boats had been sunk by convoy surface and air escorts. An even more impressive figure was that in the three months which ended in May 1943, 51 new U-boats had been added to the operational fleet while 55 had been sunk. So, for the first time, sinkings had overtaken new production. It was a distinctly healthy situation.

The victory belonged, and it is right to emphasize this once again, at least as much to the officers and men of the merchant navies as to the crews of the escorts and aircraft, the men who planned and directed operations, the scientists, the cryptographers and everyone else concerned in the battle. Merchant ships of many countries sailed in these Atlantic convoys, neutral as well as belligerent. Looking down the list of ships of a typical convoy of March 1943 (SC-122, of 51 merchant ships) one sees the flags of Britain, Greece, the Netherlands, Iceland, Norway, Panama, Sweden, the United States and Yugoslavia represented. Of nine ships sunk out of the convoy, six were British, one Dutch, one Greek and one Panamanian. Some went down with heavy loss of life.

Perhaps it is fitting that the last words on the U-boat situation at the end of May 1943 should be allowed to Admiral Dönitz. In the memoirs he wrote after the war, he observed, "The overwhelming superiority achieved by the enemy defense was finally proved beyond dispute in the operations against Convoys SC-130 and HX-239. The convoy escorts worked in exemplary harmony with the specially trained support groups. To that must be added the continuous air cover which was provided by the carrier-borne and long-range aircraft, most of them equipped with the new radar . . . Operations could only be resumed if we succeeded in radically increasing the fighting power of the U-boats. This was the logical conclusion to which I came, and accordingly I withdrew the boats from the North Atlantic. On 24 May I ordered them to proceed, using the utmost caution, to the area southwest of the Azores. We had lost the Battle of the Atlantic."

10. Return to Russia

Operation Pedestal, the convoy to Malta described in Chapter 7, put a temporary end to the regular running of convoys to North Russia, but the Allied need to do something to help the Soviet armies—and to be seen doing it—remained. The Malta convoy had been fought through in August 1942. In September another convoy to Murmansk would have to be sailed, come what may.

It was not an easy time to run a convoy. The only big carrier available, HMS *Victorious*, which had formed part of the covering force in the Mediterranean for the Pedestal convoy, was in dockyard hands for an overdue refit. The USS *Washington* with four destroyers, followed later by the heavy cruisers *Wichita* and *Tuscaloosa*, had left for other duties. Task Force 99, a most welcome addition to the British Home Fleet at a time when its strength had been much reduced through losses off Malaya and in the Mediterranean, had come to an end. That there was little enthusiasm in the fleet for a resumption of the convoy cycle to Russia was perhaps understandable in view of these reductions. But there was another reason as well. During August a medical unit and stores had been taken to North Russia in four destroyers. The purpose was to alleviate the primitive conditions in the Soviet hospitals in which sick and wounded men of the escort and merchant ships were treated. The staff and equipment were not permitted to go ashore, on direct orders from Moscow, and had to be brought back to Britain. Such a decision was hardly an encouragement to crews to try to fight another convoy through. "That British seamen, wounded while carrying supplies to Russia, should be exposed unnecessarily to the medieval treatment prevalent in Russian hospitals, was intolerable," wrote Admiral Tovey, the commander in chief of the Home Fleet, in his official dispatch.

Nevertheless, the next convoy had to sail, even though the period of perpetual northern daylight had not yet come to an end. Convoy PQ-18 consisted of 39 merchant ships, three motor minesweepers for Russia, a rescue ship and three oilers to refuel the escort ships en route. The close escort comprised two destroyers, two antiaircraft ships, two submarines and 11 corvettes, minesweepers and trawlers. The leader of the close escort was Commander A. B. Russell. The convoy was also being protected by the escort carrier *Avenger* with 12 fighters and three antisubmarine aircraft and its own private escort of two destroyers, and by 16 Home Fleet destroyers, designed as protection against attack by any of the big German

Two German submarines meet on patrol in the Arctic

surface ships now based at Narvik and Altenfjord. In overall command was Rear-Admiral Robert Burnett, flying his flag in the cruiser *Scylla*. All told, it was a formidable escort.

The Germans, too, had made their preparations for Convoy PQ-18. Eager to repeat their success against PQ-17, they had reinforced their northern air force to a strength of 92 torpedo bombers, with a similar number of high-level and dive-bombers and reconnaissance aircraft. The aircrews had been warned that, for the first time, an escort carrier would be accompanying the convoy (the German cryptographers had supplied this information). They were ordered to single her out in the initial assault. The usual numbers of U-boats were on patrol, waiting for the first air sighting of the convoy in order to deploy themselves for an all-out attack.

This sighting came on 8 September while the convoy was still north of Iceland, before the main part of its escort had joined it. Three U-boats were placed athwart its track, and four more in a line further to the eastward to form a second wave, and another five were ordered to the area. At the same time the German heavy ships *Scheer* and *Hipper*, with a cruiser and several destroyers, were moved up from Narvik to Altenfjord, so that

Heavy ships: View from the *Tirpitz* shows the *Hipper,* then the *Scheer*

they would be within easy range of the convoy's estimated route. They were seen and reported by British submarines, one of which made an unsuccessful attack, but in fact they were never used. This was on Hitler's decision, for he was still not prepared to risk surface warships that would be needed to oppose an Allied attack on Norway.

U-boats were the first to pounce. They had picked up the convoy two days after the initial air sighting and maintained contact for three days in fog, rain and snow, conditions in which it was difficult to operate aircraft from the *Avenger*. The destroyer screen had detected and attacked several contacts and sunk *U-88*, but it was unable to keep all the U-boats at a distance. Two ships were lost in a heavy attack while the convoy was west of Bear Island. About the same time PQ-18 was rediscovered by a German reconnaissance aircraft (after the first sighting north of Iceland the weather had closed in and shielded the convoy from view), and it seemed that this must be a signal for a coming attack by torpedo bombers. The shadowing aircraft were heavily armed and worked in groups of as many as nine at a time, and the *Avenger*'s Sea Hurricane fighters had little chance of driving them off. More than once the shadowers even flew low to protect the

U-boats from air attack by the *Avenger*'s Swordfish antisubmarine aircraft, engaging the latter with their automatic cannon before they could run in and release their depth charges. This was a new and disconcerting feature of the submarine battle, only made possible of course by the fact that the ice edge, even during the summer months, was still far enough south to force the convoy to sail within flying range of the German airfield at Banak.

Sure enough, the first air attacks developed that same afternoon. There were two of them, a high-level bombing attack that did no damage, and a Golden Comb with some 45 torpedo bombers, flying in line abreast 30 to 40 feet above sea level and keeping almost perfect formation 100 to 150 yards apart. "They were like a huge flight of nightmare locusts," wrote Rear Admiral Boddam-Whetham, the convoy's commodore, and as he saw them coming he ordered the convoy to make an emergency turn of 45° toward them. The two wing columns failed to obey the order, or perhaps had not enough time to execute it, since the whole attack lasted only eight minutes. The aircraft, each carrying two torpedoes, flew on through the intense barrage from every gun in the escorts and the merchant ships, and the survivors dropped their torpedoes within 2,000 yards. Six of the seven ships in the two wing columns which had failed to turn were hit and sunk; two others in the middle of the convoy were also sunk as the other torpedoes ran through—eight ships in all, and at a cost of only five aircraft shot down. There were attacks later, but they were half-hearted affairs compared with the earlier Golden Comb. No ships in the convoy were hit and three of the torpedo bombers were shot down, making a total of eight aircraft for the day.

It was obvious that the carrier had not earned her keep on this day's fighting. She had been flying off her fighters to try to drive the shadowers away, and when the torpedo bombers arrived the fighters had used up all their ammunition and could only make feint attacks on the enemy. The captain of the *Avenger*, Commander Colthurst, decided to change his tactics. He would ignore the shadowers, which in any case were too heavily armed to be driven off by the already obsolete Sea Hurricanes, and would keep sections of aircraft aloft continuously throughout the day. At least two would always be ready to pounce on any attackers.

During the night one ship was sunk by a U-boat, but she was avenged in the morning when *U-589* was sunk by HMS *Onslow,* one of the destroyer escorts. Later the torpedo bombers came in, dividing into two groups, one of which made a dead set at the *Avenger* and the other at the *Scylla,* Admiral Burnett's flagship. This was a change in tactics, for the targets now were the escort ships. The merchantmen were ignored. The *Avenger* left her station in the convoy and, accompanied by her screen of two destroyers, steamed out into open water ahead in order to have room to maneuver and fly off her fighters. "It was a fine sight," wrote Admiral

HMS *Biter*, a sister ship of the escort carrier *Avenger*

Burnett, "to see the *Avenger* peeling off Hurricanes whilst streaking across the front of the convoy from starboard to port inside the screen with her destroyer escort blazing away with any gun which would bear, and then being chased by torpedo bombers as she steamed down on the opposite course to the convoy to take cover." The *Avenger* flew off six fighters, and the new plan of operation worked. No ship was hit and the Germans lost 11 aircraft.

There were more attacks to come, mainly from high-level bombers which tried to drop their bombs through holes in the clouds. They had no success, but one dive-bomber nearly hit the *Avenger*. Then the torpedo bombers returned, 25 of them; their chief target was again the *Avenger*, which was operating clear of the convoy. By the time they arrived she had 10 fighters in the air, and they and the ships' guns shot down nine of the enemy. The *Avenger* was not hit, but a stray torpedo sank a merchantman which, loaded with ammunition and high explosives, blew up when the torpedo exploded. "It is a funny feeling," wrote the convoy commodore, "to realize one is sitting on top of 2,000 tons of TNT, but we nearly all carry between that and 4,000 tons. I don't think the bigger amount would make more than some tiny fraction of a second difference to the time one entered the next world."

There was little more to follow, for the convoy was getting well into the Barents Sea. Apart from attempts at high-level bombing, all of which were unsuccessful, only U-boats were left to face. Three of them were in actual contact with the convoy, though the heavy escort kept them outside torpedo range; another 12 were in the vicinity. None had any success, and *U-457* was sunk by the destroyer *Impulsive*.

By now PQ-18 was close to its destination, and on the arrival of two Soviet destroyers to help bring it in, Admiral Burnett left with his ships to take over the return convoy, QP-14, which was just setting sail. But before PQ-18 made port, German torpedo bombers launched two final attacks, coming in low from astern. One more ship was sunk at the cost of four aircraft.

The Luftwaffe was disappointed with the results. They had made somewhat more than 100 attacks with torpedo bombers and somewhat fewer than 100 with high-level and dive-bombers, and they had sunk 10 ships with torpedoes. The Luftwaffe War Diary recorded that "it was found not only that it was impossible to approach the aircraft carrier to launch an effective attack—on account of the fighters—but that a wide screen of warships made the launching of torpedoes against the inner merchant vessels an extremely hazardous undertaking. Aircraft losses were heavy . . ." They in fact totaled 41, of which 33 were torpedo bombers.

The attacks on PQ-18, and on the returning convoy, QP-14, turned out to be the high-water mark of German attempts to stop the convoys to North Russia. Before the next convoys sailed there had to be a break in the cycle while the Allies mounted Operation Torch, the invasion of North Africa, in November 1942. The Germans switched strength, too. All their torpedo bombers based in Norway were hurriedly transferred to the Mediterranean, leaving only a few dive-bombers and long-range reconnaissance aircraft to threaten the next convoys. The main foes now were to be the U-boats and the warships still stationed in Norwegian bases, of which the major units were the *Tirpitz, Lützow, Hipper, Köln* and *Nürnberg*. For security reasons the convoy nomenclature was changed, convoys to Russia being known as JW, those to England as RA. Both series started with the number 51. The first JW convoy left in mid-December 1942, and it sailed against a new background of hope and confidence.

All had gone well in North Africa. The Battle of Alamein had been fought and won, and Field Marshal Rommel and his armies, German and Italian, had been driven back nearly 1,000 miles from the Egyptian border. On the other side of the continent the Anglo-American army commanded by General Eisenhower had advanced quickly through Morocco and Algeria and was battering on the border of Tunisia, the last of the German-occupied areas in Africa. The Soviet winter offensive was under way, and Stalingrad, with its German Sixth Army of 330,000 men, was invested and would shortly fall. In the Pacific the Americans had recovered their breath after the first tremendous Japanese onslaught, had won the campaign for Guadalcanal and were now at the start of their victorious advance up the

Pacific islands which was finally to end at Tokyo. All the signs were hopeful. And in the Arctic, as these convoys restarted, it was the season when almost perpetual darkness would provide a measure of protection against the assaults of the U-boats and the attentions of shadowing aircraft. Only in the Atlantic did the old sores still fester, with the U-boats and the Luftwaffe still taking a frightening toll of merchant ships.

Convoy JW-51 was sailed in two parts, A and B, the reason being that in the winter blizzards and snowstorms it was easier to keep a small number of ships in compact formation than a large one. This meant, of course, halving the usual escort. Each group sailed with a close escort of about seven destroyers, with a covering force of two cruisers and two destroyers. JW-51A completed its voyage without trouble, unsighted by the enemy throughout its passage. JW-51B sailed from Scotland on 22 December and, after being somewhat scattered by a heavy gale and thick weather, was sighted and reported by *U-354* on 30 December when it was 50 miles south of Bear Island, with two merchant ships still straggling and a destroyer and minesweeper looking for them. The cruiser force, commanded by the same Rear Admiral Burnett who had taken PQ-18 through,

Band welcomes a U-boat on its return to Trondheim, Norway

Hipper lies at anchor in a Norwegian fjord

was to the south of the convoy. The close escort consisted of five destroyers, led by Captain R. St. V. Sherbrooke in the *Onslow*, and two corvettes. Realizing that the convoy had been sighted by a U-boat and reported, Admiral Burnett took his cruisers up slightly to the north of the position where he reckoned the convoy to be "in order to gain the advantage of light over any enemy that might appear." He was obviously anticipating an attack by German surface forces from Altenfjord and calculating that the earliest they could arrive would be the morning of 31 December. It would have been an excellent position for a fight if the convoy was where he thought it was. In fact, however, the weather had slowed it down and it was about 150 miles to the westward and 20 miles to the southward of where it was thought to be.

The U-boat's sighting report had indicated that JW-51B was weakly protected, and Vice-Admiral Kummetz, the German Flag Officer, Norway, wasted no time in sailing from Altenfjord with the pocket battleship *Lützow*, the heavy cruiser *Hipper* and six destroyers, aiming for a point in the Barents Sea on the convoy's expected route about 200 miles east of Bear Island. He did not know of the presence of Admiral Burnett's cruiser force; all he expected to find were a few destroyers round the convoy. And he was, to some extent, hamstrung with orders not to risk his ships, one of them being that he was not to attack at night for fear of the escort's torpedoes. Moreover, he was given a secondary aim—to see the *Lützow* on her way into the Atlantic to operate as a commerce raider after the attack on the convoy. With two separate and unrelated operations to perform at the same time, his hands were to some extent tied. Admiral Kummetz's plan was to divide his force in two and attack the convoy from astern simultaneously from both sides. He took the *Hipper* and three destroyers to the north of the convoy, leaving the *Lützow* and the other three destroyers to the south. As it turned out, it was a plan which would have annihilated the convoy but for the caution (or timidity) of Captain Stange of the *Lützow*, who at one time had the convoy at his mercy.

New Year's Eve dawned with the Arctic in relatively mild mood. The visibility was about 10 miles to the southward and seven miles to the northward, which was the "advantage of light" anticipated by Admiral Burnett. Apart from occasional snow showers, which of course temporarily cut down the visibility, the weather was clear and the sea slight. There were 16 degrees of frost, and ice had formed on all ships. The convoy itself was about 240 miles southeast of Bear Island and about the same distance from its destination. Admiral Burnett's cruisers were about 30 miles north of it, with a straggler being escorted by a trawler another 15 miles to the north. The minesweeper *Bramble*, looking for a straggler, was out on her own about 15 miles northeast of the convoy. None of the four groups knew exactly where the others were, and none knew that the German surface ships were at sea. By 8:30 A.M. the *Hipper* had crossed the wake of JW-51B and was some 16 miles to the northwestward, while the *Lützow*, still about 50 miles from the convoy, was closing in from the south.

It was at this moment that one of the screening destroyers reported sighting two destroyers. Ordered to investigate, she soon sighted a third. These were the three with the *Hipper*, opening out to form a line of search before sweeping to the eastward for the convoy. On being sighted they turned away and were chased for an hour, with a brief engagement, before the British destroyer returned to the convoy. Meanwhile, having seen the gun flashes, Captain Sherbrooke turned the *Onslow* toward them, signaling to another destroyer, the *Orwell*, to join him. But before he could reach the enemy he sighted a far more formidable opponent, which he eventually recognized as the *Hipper*. Ordering the other destroyers of the escort to lay in a smoke screen round the convoy, Sherbrooke took the *Onslow* and *Orwell* in to engage the *Hipper*, driving her northward, away from the convoy. This development was probably part of Admiral Kummetz's plan—to draw the escort away and leave the convoy open and unguarded for the *Lützow*. The two destroyers claimed three hits on the *Hipper* (the German records make no mention of these) before she turned and fought back. She hit the *Onslow* four times, putting two guns out of action and causing considerable damage. Captain Sherbrooke was severely wounded in the face and temporarily blinded, but he continued to direct the battle until another hit on the ship forced him to disengage, when he turned over the

137

command to Lieutenant-Commander Kinloch of the *Orwell*. Only then did he leave the bridge of his ship for medical treatment, and as he did so, the *Hipper* disappeared in a snowstorm. Sherbrooke was awarded the Victoria Cross for his valor in this action.

Meanwhile Admiral Burnett, who had received the *Onslow's* enemy reports, was coming down from the north with his two cruisers. As they ran to the south they came in sight of the gun flashes of the engagement between the two British destroyers and the *Hipper*. Burnett had been delayed because of a radar contact which he decided to investigate—it turned out to be a straggler from the convoy—and as a result was later than expected on the scene of battle. The action between the *Hipper* and the destroyers was over by the time he reached the position, but a radar contact at a range of 19,000 yards appeared hopeful, and the cruisers began to close in.

In the meantime the convoy had been ordered to make an emergency turn to the south away from the *Hipper*, and the two British destroyers which had been engaging her and those laying the smoke screens were hurrying back to it. A report of smoke to the southward came in from one of the two corvettes of the escort, followed 10 minutes later with an amplification that it was a large ship crossing ahead of the convoy. This was the *Lützow* and her destroyers, though she was not identified; she was no more than two miles away. Just at that moment a heavy snow squall blotted out most of the convoy from the *Lützow's* sight. Captain Stange decided that it would be unwise to open fire. He did not know the exact positions of the escorts, and he was unwilling to risk an attack by their torpedoes. He decided to stand off and wait for a clearance in the weather.

Having at last reached the convoy, the British destroyers passed ahead of it and sighted a large ship, which was taken to be the *Hipper*. It was in fact the *Lützow*, which no one on the British side yet knew was at sea. The destroyers steered between her and the convoy so as to form a shield. At the same time the *Hipper* came into view and opened fire on the destroyer *Achates*, which was coming up to join those trying to herd off the *Lützow*. She was hit by a heavy shell which crippled her and killed her captain and 40 of her crew. The *Hipper* then switched her fire to the other destroyers. Suddenly she was herself hit three times, from a totally unexpected direction. The fire came from Admiral Burnett's cruisers, just arrived. Admiral Kummetz thus found himself between cruisers to the north and destroyers to the south and, fearing a torpedo attack, turned away to win clear. The move brought him closer to the cruisers. The range was down to 8,000 yards, when a fortunate snow squall suddenly shielded the *Hipper* from view. It was all too much for Kummetz, and he made a signal calling off the whole operation and ordering his ships to return to base.

But the fighting was not yet completely over. As the Germans tried to disengage to the westward, one of the *Hipper's* escorting destroyers, the

Friedrich Eckoldt, came within range of the cruisers. She was reduced to a wreck within 10 minutes, and later sank. The *Lützow,* now nine miles to the north of the convoy, fired a few shots at it as she made her way to join up with the *Hipper.* One merchant ship was damaged. The British destroyers closed the pocket battleship, opening fire on her as they hastened her away from the convoy, and the cruisers joined in the chase. There was a little long-range firing as the whole German force sped away for home, but no more hits were made on either side. The convoy, with the one ship damaged by the *Lützow's* shell, reached Russia in safety, but the *Achates,* with her bows deep in the water and a list of 60° after the damage caused by the *Hipper,* capsized in the afternoon. Her remaining crew of 81 were saved by one of the trawlers with the convoy.

It had been a good day for the British. They had lost one destroyer but had in return sunk a larger one. The convoy had come through without loss, apart from some damage to one ship from a shell burst. As Admiral Tovey later wrote in his report, "that an enemy force of at least one pocket battleship, one heavy cruiser, and six destroyers, with all the advantage of surprise and concentration, should be held off for four hours by five

The battle cruiser *Scharnhorst* hides in Norwegian shadows

Admiral Fraser greets U.S. Navy Secretary Frank Knox aboard the *Duke of York*

destroyers and driven from the area by two 6-inch cruisers without any loss to the convoy is most creditable and satisfactory." Captain Stange, of the *Lützow*, recorded his feelings in his War Diary: "As we withdrew from the scene of action, the unsatisfactory feeling reigned that in spite of the general position, which was apparently favorable at first, we had not succeeded at getting at the convoy or in scoring any successes at all." And he should have known, for at one time during the action, if he had gone in boldly, he could have sunk a number of ships almost without risk to himself.

It is not difficult to find the reasons for this success, even though it may appear something of a paradox. The initiative was entirely in the hands of the German ships; they had the superiority of weight of gunfire (11-inch guns in the *Lützow*, 8-inch in the *Hipper*) and the opportunity to wipe out the convoy and its escort before the British cruisers could arrive on the scene. But their tactics throughout were defensive, especially at those moments during the battle when offense would have brought them the prize they desired. The convoy escorts, whose role was always to defend their charges, did so invariably and effectively by taking the offensive, placing themselves between the enemy ships and the convoy and driving them away every time.

The next few convoys went through without much trouble, even the U-boats appearing to be disheartened by the losses they incurred while attempting to attack. In the main they were intercepted by escort forces, or by aircraft from an escort carrier, long before they could reach a good firing position, and though their losses were never cripplingly heavy, little or nothing came their way in exchange. In April, as the period of permanent daylight was approaching, the urgent needs of the Atlantic battle called for every destroyer that could be spared. For a time the convoys to Russia were suspended, to be resumed later in the year when the darkness returned.

The next convoy against which the Germans operated surface ships was JW-55B. It sailed almost exactly a year later, on 20 December 1943. It was expected to pass south of Bear Island on Christmas Day. As close escort it had eight modern destroyers commanded by Captain J. A. McCoy, two elderly World War I destroyers, two corvettes and a minesweeper. Three cruisers under Admiral Burnett were to provide extra cover in the vicinity of Bear Island, and distant cover was provided by the Commander in Chief, Admiral Sir Bruce Fraser, in the battleship *Duke of York*, with a cruiser and four destroyers.

Although the Germans were well aware that the convoys to North Russia had restarted, they were reluctant to use surface forces against them because of the effectiveness of British radar. There had been much talk in high circles in Berlin of the apparent uselessness of the German heavy warships, and suggestions had been made to lay them up, mount their big guns ashore and retrain their crews for U-boat warfare. Admiral Dönitz, who had now succeeded to overall command of the German Navy, wished to demonstrate to Hitler that this sort of talk was defeatist, bad for naval morale, and asked the Führer to allow him to use the battle cruiser *Scharnhorst* against the Arctic convoys to prove her value in this sort of warfare. Permission was granted on 19 December, and the order went northward from Berlin to sail the battle cruiser against the next convoy. This was JW-55B. It was sighted and reported by a U-boat on the morning of 25 December, and the *Scharnhorst,* with five destroyers in company, was sailed from Altenfjord that same evening. Almost immediately they ran into heavy seas, so bad at times that the destroyers could not keep up. Rear Admiral Bey, in command of operation, suggested calling it off on account of the destroyers' loss of fighting efficiency in such weather, but Dönitz ordered him to continue, even if the destroyers could not remain at sea and the *Scharnhorst* had to go it alone. This order left Bey with no choice. He pushed on through the night, well supplied with information about the convoy's progress from the eight U-boats which were now in contact and shadowing.

On the morning of the 26th, JW-55B was south of Bear Island. Admiral Burnett's cruisers were coming toward it from the northeast, and the *Scharnhorst* and her destroyers were approaching rapidly from the south. Bey spread his destroyers on a line of search, and they were out of sight of *Scharnhorst* when, unawares, she came within radar range of the British cruisers. She was taken completely by surprise, and quickly hit. Using her superior speed, she disappeared to the northeast. Thinking that she was now intending to attack the convoy from the north, Admiral Burnett steamed in that direction to place his cruisers between the battle cruiser and the convoy.

They met again, and after another exchange of gunfire in which hits were made by both sides, the *Scharnhorst* broke off the action and made for home on a southerly course, followed and continually shadowed by Admiral Burnett's cruisers. Still unknown to Admiral Bey, the *Duke of York* was down to the southeast and by now steering a course to intercept. The cruisers drove the enemy battle cruiser onto her guns. The rest is history. Later that evening the *Scharnhorst* was sent to the bottom by the massed guns and torpedoes of battleship, cruisers and destroyers.

The convoy thus escaped, but only just. After the *Scharnhorst's* destroyers had failed to find the convoy on their first sweep, Admiral Bey had ordered them to make a second sweep to the westward. They passed less than eight miles south of the convoy during their run to the westward but failed to sight it, and on completion of the sweep Admiral Bey ordered them to return to their base at Altenfjord. JW-55B continued on its way to Russia after this narrow escape and arrived there without loss.

With the sinking of the *Scharnhorst*, the only bar to the passage of the Arctic convoys was the presence of U-boats. The only other large German warship in the north was the *Tirpitz*, and she was out of action as the result of damage inflicted by carrier-borne aircraft. The U-boats were held in check by the very large destroyer escorts which were sailed with these convoys—JW-57, for example, a convoy of 42 merchant ships and six Soviet small craft, had an escort of no fewer than 33 Home Fleet warships, including cruisers, destroyers, frigates and corvettes—and only toward the very end of the war did they ever again constitute a real threat. By that time the snorkel-fitted U-boats, which could operate continually submerged and were immune from radar detection, were gathered in large numbers in the waters off the Kola Inlet, the usual destination of the convoys to North Russia. The limited sea room in this area meant that the U-boat concentration could not be avoided. Every convoy was forced to fight its way through. By this time, too, with the fighting over in the Mediterranean, German torpedo bombers had been brought back to northern Norway, though not in the large numbers available in 1942.

These conditions made some losses inevitable—losses that somehow were always a bit more poignant when they occurred at the end of a voyage across the Arctic and so near to safety. But there were also U-boats sunk and aircraft shot down to add to the other side of the balance sheet. The operation of the Arctic convoys continued right up to the end of the war; in fact, the last one, JW-67, sailed from the Clyde, Scotland, on 12 May 1945, four days after V-E Day.

Guns of the *Scharnhorst*—a 5.9-inch secondary battery

These convoys to North Russia were an unforgettable experience to anyone who sailed in them. As formidable as the danger from U-boats, aircraft and surface ships was the weather, and the damage it could do to ships. Gales of intense violence were commonplace. Often they were accompanied by snow squalls of such thickness that even a ship in the middle of a convoy seemed to sail alone in a white wilderness. Ships with holds filled with explosives and other war stores carried deck cargoes of tanks, trucks and locomotives, and a gale could cause these to shift, necessitating a lonely return to harbor. Even worse, perhaps, was the plight of the homeward-bound convoys. Since there was little cargo to carry home from the Soviet Union, they sailed with their sterns ballasted down to keep their propellers in the water and their bows riding high. In a gale they became almost unmanageable. Escorts as well as merchant ships suffered in such weather, losing boats, deck gear and sometimes even members of the crew. A man overboard had little chance of survival. Often the sea was so high that a boat could not be launched. Even if rescue were attempted the cold generally killed him before he could be reached.

Ice, too, was a perpetual danger. Iceblink and a sudden drop in temperature usually gave warning of approach to a large floe or the ice edge. Smaller floes were difficult to detect, and they could do much damage to bows, rudders and propellers. There were temptations at times to try to escape U-boat attack by entering the ice leads, but a ship that did so would find that it had entered a blind alley, with the ice closing in behind her. As experience of these convoys grew, most of the escorts, and with them the merchant ships, preferred to accept all the hazards of U-boat attack in open water rather than get entangled in the ice.

Ice and snow on board were additional hazards. They increased in bulk very quickly if left untouched. A daily exercise on all ships was to turn the hands to chipping away ice and snow with pickaxes and heavy hammers. Later, steam hoses were used to shift the ice. But a ship which neglected to clear the ice from her decks and top-hamper would quickly become unstable. The additional weight would render her liable to capsize when the gales blew and the sea rose.

The final balance sheet was impressive, even though the cost in men and ships had been high. The total value of the material shipped to Russia in these Arctic convoys amounted to more than $2 billion, and the total

Tirpitz wears an elaborate disguise to mislead unwanted visitors

tonnage carried was more than 4,000,000—including 5,000 tanks and more than 7,000 aircraft. In the 40 outward-bound convoys the number of merchant ships sailed was 811, of which 720 reached their destination; 58 were sunk, and 33 had to turn back for various reasons. The loss of life in the British and Allied merchant navies was 829 officers and men. Of the escort forces 18 ships of the Royal Navy and one Polish-manned submarine were sunk, with an overall loss of 1,815 officers and men; another 129 were killed in action with enemy ships and aircraft. The enemy, too, suffered heavy losses. The battle cruiser *Scharnhorst* went down with almost the whole of her crew of some 2,000 men. Three large destroyers, 38 U-boats and an unknown number of aircraft were destroyed in action, and few of their crews can have survived. The cost of the German successes, too, had been high.

11. Cornered

When Admiral Dönitz ordered the withdrawal of all U-boats from the North Atlantic on 24 May 1943, he may have been down but he was certainly not yet out. He knew that the North Atlantic was the vital area in the overall Battle of the Atlantic. He must be able completely to dominate that area if Germany was to have any chance at all of winning the war. For the time being the North Atlantic had been made too hot for his U-boats, but eventually he would have to try once more to cut that most vital trade route. While his U-boats were reequipping for a renewal of their onslaught in those waters there might well be some useful dividends to be gathered on the more southerly supply routes, which the Americans used to nourish the Mediterranean campaign. These operations would only be peripheral to the main task, but they served to keep alive and in good order the skill and morale of the submarine crews.

Dönitz had originally expected that the U-boats would be ready to return to the North Atlantic in July 1943, but in fact it turned out to be 13 September before he felt justified in giving the order. Always in the forefront of his mind was the need to provide the U-boats with some effective counter to the air escort which had so plagued them round the convoys, forcing them to submerge and lose contact just as the prospects of a mass

146

Vice Admiral Patrick Bellinger, air commander of the U.S. Atlantic Fleet

attack looked most promising. The admiral thought he had found the answer in a four-barreled antiaircraft gun which could be fitted on the "winter garden," the small, circular bandstand just abaft the submarine's bridge. With this gun a U-boat could fight back at an aircraft while remaining on the surface. But production was slow. The next best weapon was an automatic 20-mm gun, with which in the end most of the submarines were fitted.

The next requirement was an improved radar search receiver to give a U-boat's crew audible warning of an enemy radar contact. Dönitz's scientists came up with the Hagenuk receiver, but it was no more successful than the Metox in recording a centimetric pulse. U-boats were also supplied with Aphrodite radar decoy balloons, designed to mislead convoy escorts, but these, too, had little success.

The most important new weapon was the Zaunkönig (Wren) torpedo—contemptuously christened "Gnat" by the British—which had a built-in acoustic homing device in its guidance system. It was designed to home in on escorts rather than on merchant ships, on the theory that a preliminary reduction in the number of escorts would later make easier a subsequent mass attack on the sheep. This was a departure from the U-boat tactics of the past four years, where the primary target had been merchant ships. It may well be that, at least until the end of 1942, the general shortage of escorts had led the Germans to believe that they were not worth the cost of a torpedo when there were so many fatter targets available and easier to hit. Actually, however, substantial escort losses in the early years of the Atlantic battle would certainly have presented almost insuperable difficulties of convoy protection. Now the change of tactics had come too late. The new frigates, sloops and corvettes were coming out of the builders' yards in a flood. And the Gnat had only a limited success. Allied scientists soon produced an answer in the shape of the Foxer, a noise-making machine, towed behind the escorts, which attracted the Gnats clear of the escort ships' propellers.

Another stroke of ill fortune came Dönitz's way at this time. It had become apparent to the Allies in June 1943 that the naval code—in which the daily convoy signal, the rerouting instructions to individual convoys and much other interesting information was signaled—was being decrypted in Germany. Now new Allied ciphers were introduced, and they baffled the German cryptographers for the remainder of the war. Gone forever was the magnificent source of information on which Dönitz had been able to plan his U-boat attacks. At the same time, as a result of suspicions expressed in the U-boat headquarters, an inquiry was held in Germany into the possibility of an Allied break of the Enigma cipher, but so confident were the Germans of the invincibility of their system that Enigma was given a clean bill of health. U-boats continued to use the Triton cipher in the Atlantic. Thus what was denied to Dönitz was still available to the trackers in London.

The admiral's signal to the U-boats on 13 September 1943 informed them that "all the essentials of a successful campaign are at hand," and ordered the opening of a new campaign in the North Atlantic. It was not long before they found their first target. On 19 September the usual flurry of radio transmissions indicated to the Tracking Room in London that a convoy was being reported and shadowed. Direction-finding bearings showed the target to be either Convoy ON-202, of 38 ships with seven escorts, or ONS-18, of 27 ships with eight escorts and a merchant aircraft carrier. The two convoys were close together, and a signal was sent from London ordering them to merge. At the same time a support group of five antisubmarine vessels was ordered to join them. All these moves had been completed by dusk on 20 September. Air cover was given, whenever conditions were suitable for flying, by shore-based VLR aircraft and by the MAC ship's Swordfish.

A pack of 19 U-boats attacked that night, when there was no escort. Next morning they claimed to have sunk 12 escort ships and nine merchant ships. The actual casualties were three escorts and six merchantmen, at a cost of two German submarines sunk and two severely damaged. Accepting his U-boats' claims as accurate, Dönitz ordered his wolf packs to keep concentrating on escort ships before going for the merchantmen. But within two or three weeks the Foxer had been devised, produced and supplied to escort ships, and once again a massacre of U-boats took place in the North Atlantic. Perhaps typical of this stage of the battle was an attack by about 15 submarines on Convoy SC-143. The pack attacked for three days between 7 and 9 October, less than a month after Dönitz had ordered the renewal of operations in the North Atlantic, and managed to sink one escort ship out of the 12 guarding the convoy and only one merchant ship out of the total of 39. German losses were three U-boats, all sent to the bottom by escorting aircraft, which also consistently put down the surfaced U-boats attempting to get into good firing positions for subsequent attack. In the U-boat headquarters War Diary for 1 November 1943 was the entry, "We cannot stand these losses, particularly with no successes to counterbalance them." This was a statement of fact, and it forced Dönitz into introducing new tactics designed to avoid such crippling losses.

Here the admiral found himself on the horns of an almost insuperable dilemma. To earn their keep, U-boats had to attack the convoys. Otherwise they might just as well not be in the Atlantic at all. Once a convoy had been located, contact must be kept and reported frequently to enable a wolf pack to be assembled for a large-scale attack. Since the average speed of a convoy was about nine knots, a U-boat had to be able to use her surface speed by day to keep up and shadow, for her submerged speed was much too low. But continuous daylight escort by aircraft meant that every U-boat on the surface within a dozen miles of a convoy—about the maximum visibility distance for shadowing in good conditions—was certain to be attacked from the air with the more sophisticated weapons now

149

available—depth charges with shallow explosion settings and homing torpedoes. Where lay the answer?

The U-boats were now having to work in total darkness. Since the introduction of the new Allied ciphers the B-dienst had been able to tell Dönitz nothing about the dates convoys would sail and the routes they would take. No longer could he assemble a pack of U-boats in a position where he could be reasonably sure that, in due course, a victim would appear. This meant inevitably that he must abandon his whole wolf-pack philosophy and instead scatter his U-boats in small groups over as wide an area of the Atlantic as possible. Further, because of the menace of the air escorts, they must remain submerged by day, coming to the surface only at night to recharge their batteries and perhaps gaining a haphazard sighting of a convoy.

As if these were not difficulties enough, Dönitz now had another headache. The U-tankers, by means of which operational U-boats had been able to prolong their patrols in distant areas by refueling in mid-ocean, had proved vulnerable to attack. They had been driven from the North Atlantic, though still operating further south in the vicinity of the Cape Verde Islands. They had been hunted down and sunk mainly by the support groups operating with a carrier, frequently with the assistance of intelligence gained from the cracking of the Enigma cipher. Combined with this were constant Allied air patrols covering the main exits into the ocean from the U-boat bases—the Shetlands-Faeroes gap from the Norwegian bases and the Bay of Biscay from the French bases. For a time Dönitz had ordered his submarines to transit these two exits on the surface and fight it out with attacking aircraft, but losses had been heavy. As a result, the orders had been reversed, and the U-boats now ran submerged, surfacing only to recharge their batteries. Where in the early days of the war a U-boat could reach a patrol area in the eastern Atlantic in three or four days, it now took them 11 or 12 days to make the same passage. Their time on patrol was thus considerably reduced.

Dönitz's new plan was to enlist the help of the Luftwaffe. Its fliers would find the convoys and report their positions and movements so that U-boats could be concentrated in the vicinity. The 20-mm antiaircraft gun was to be replaced by a heavier 37-mm automatic gun, as an inducement to remain on the surface when intercepted by aircraft, and U-boat captains were told to attempt undetected attacks on convoys by coming up from a-stern instead of lying in wait ahead of them. In a message to the U-boats at sea on 13 November, Dönitz said, "From today the first four-engined long-distance reconnaissance Ju 290s are available for operations, having a radius of action of 1,400 sea miles. Both their number and their radius will be increased . . . The difficulties of attacking the surface escorts are materially reduced by the use of the acoustic torpedo. The effectiveness of pursuit with depth charges has fallen off, and the enemy has become less confident

Mousetrap—a lightweight, rocket version
of Hedgehog

and less determined. In dealing with the main enemy—the air force—the 3.7-cm automatic gun will further ease the situation and will give the U-boat more freedom of movement in daylight. It has already been installed in seven boats . . . The failure last month in the Atlantic [12 merchant ships of 56,422 tons sunk at a cost of 23 U-boats] was due to not finding the convoys." The submarines themselves were stationed in small groups along the expected routes, where they awaited a call from the aircraft. They remained submerged by day to avoid aircraft attack, only surfacing at night when air escort, they hoped, was quiescent.

Inevitably, as a matter of geography, the main thrust of German air reconnaissance was directed against the U.K.-Gibraltar convoys, which were most easily reached from Luftwaffe airfields in western France. In turn, more U-boats came down from the North Atlantic to cooperate with the aircraft in southern latitudes, making even safer the passages of the vital North Atlantic convoys. But life was not easy for the U-boats in these waters, either. Portugal, Britain's oldest ally, had given permission for an Allied air base to be set up in the Azores. Some of the aircraft were fitted with a Leigh Light for night operations, so that air escort could now be provided round the clock. Also, more than enough escort carriers were in commission to provide one for every convoy crossing the Atlantic. They were equipped with night as well as day fighters to keep the German reconnaissance aircraft at bay.

A despairing note began to creep into Dönitz's signals to his U-boats. "In the most recent convoy operations," he informed them on 28 December, "it has happened again and again that the convoy swept past the U-boats, who were unable to exploit the unique opportunity to attack and found themselves lagging hopelessly astern of the target. Moreover, numerous recent unsuccessful submerged attacks have shown that often the U-boats can no longer penetrate the screen without being located while at periscope depth by enemy asdics [sonar] or hydrophones, We must therefore face the prospect of abandoning attacks at periscope depth and adopting more and more the blind firing method from a greater depth, using the new types of torpedoes designed for this purpose." This message was really no more than whistling in the dark, for the "new types of torpedoes" never did make their appearance.

With this new and wide dispersion of U-boats, coupled with the consequent reduction in the number of convoys threatened by massed attack, it became possible to use some of the support groups as independent "hunter-killer" groups. The U.S. Navy operated four of these groups, each based on an escort carrier, and they had a very considerable success. They worked mainly in the southern half of the North Atlantic, and many of their kills came as a result of U-boat positions gained from decrypted signals. Some concern, in fact, was expressed in Britain at the considerable use made of this decrypted material by the groups centered on the escort car-

USS *Philadelphia* on escort duty

riers *Bogue, Santee, Card* and *Core,* on the ground that the Germans might suspect that their Enigma cipher had been compromised, but in this particular case fortune favored the brave and German confidence in their cipher remained unshaken.

A typical example of the work of a support group at this period of the Atlantic battle is provided by the cruise of a British group, based on the escort carriers *Nairana* and *Activity,* at the beginning of 1944. It was commanded by Captain F. J. Walker, who had made himself the most proficient U-boat killer in the Royal Navy. For its first week in the North Atlantic, the group had no convoy to guard, and it found no U-boats until the last day, when *U-592* was destroyed while trying to attack the *Nairana.* Walker was then ordered to support the surface escort of Convoys SL-147/KMS-38, which were threatened with attack. Shortly after his group reached the convoy, *U-762* was sighted and quickly sunk. A few hours later, *U-734* joined her on the bottom. A DF bearing from the convoy led the group to *U-238* and she was sent to join her sisters. Next day, in a search to the northwestward, the support group contacted and destroyed *U-424.* Walker was then sent to join Convoy HX-278, which escaped attack, and three days later was with Convoy ON-224, in the vicinity of which a U-boat had been reported. Sweeping back along the convoy's route, the group found *U-264* and sent her to the bottom in a swift attack. The total bag in this one 27-day cruise was six U-boats.

Captain Walker, whom we met when the *Audacity*, the first of the merchant aircraft carriers, was operational in 1941, became something of a legend in the Royal Navy. He had worked out a new tactic which he called a "creeping" attack. After a U-boat was detected by sonar he stationed ships of his support group to "keep the ring." They followed every movement of the submarine with their sonars and drove it back into the center with depth charges whenever it was detected trying to break clear. Two of the group kept in the center and, as opportunity offered, made devastating attacks with patterns of from 10 to 14 depth charges each. Very few targets ever escaped this form of attack. Since the group had no convoy commitment as close escort, it could always afford the time to hunt the U-boat to destruction, and in at least one case it stayed with a U-boat for 16 hours before it was finally blown to the surface by depth charges and sunk by gunfire. All told, during the 21 months of its existence this support group sank no fewer than 23 U-boats.

There was no question now in anyone's mind, Allied or German, that the combination of continuous air escort and support group had effectively destroyed the whole basis of Dönitz's strategy in the Atlantic. Gone forever

Escort carrier USS *Card*

was the night attack on a convoy by surfaced U-boats; gone forever, too, was the organization of groups of U-boats into coordinated wolf packs. Other difficulties, perhaps small in themselves but considerable in their cumulative effect, began to pile up and further sap the waning confidence of U-boat captains. The Type VIIC 507-ton U-boats, which formed the backbone of the fleet, had become top-heavy. The heavier antiaircraft armament added to the weight of the armored bridge produced at times a roll of as much as 60°, and a very moderate sea produced a continuous roll of up to 30° each side. The physical strain of such movement on the crews was considerable, and visibility was considerably reduced. Both of these factors tended to reduce a crew's efficiency. Other problems of a similar nature added to the general discomfiture.

Admiral Dönitz's new tactical orders were hardly helpful. They assumed that a U-boat in contact with a convoy would be able to come to the surface "and, after making an enemy report, haul ahead . . . All boats that are in a favorable position when a sighting report is received from a U-boat are to stalk the enemy by day and night . . ." How this was to be done in the face of air escort—and every convoy on the ocean now had air escort—was not explained. The final paragraph of the new tactical orders must have confused the U-boat captains even further. "Whenever in the operational area the U-boats register enemy radar activity," it ran, "they dive on the assumption that they have been located from the air. After diving, the boats' hydrophones will often establish that the pursuer is in fact a destroyer or a corvette, which will by then be nearing the diving position. By then it will be too late to surface, and the boat is forced onto the defensive and will usually have to suffer a depth-charge attack. If because of such experience the boat, when next located by the enemy, decides to remain on the surface, that also will be wrong, for a bombing attack from the air is likely to follow." Dönitz himself might well be tossed upon the horns of a dilemma, but tactical remarks such as these must have faced his captains with a dilemma of considerably greater proportions. The final result of all this indecision was that the U-boats were disposed across the Atlantic in individual patrol areas of about 20 to 40 miles broad, between the general latitudes of 48°N and 61°N. They remained submerged by day and came to the surface at night. This dispersion was the entire negation of any form of integrated attack on a convoy, and in fact whenever a submarine did locate a convoy it became a fugitive and hunted foe, more often than not doomed to destruction. The figures for the first five months of 1944 tell the story: 19 ships of 119,733 tons sunk in the North Atlantic at a cost of 50 U-boats. And this was exactly one year after the Allies themselves had been facing almost certain defeat in the Atlantic. This turn of the wheel of fortune was cataclysmic for Germany, for ever since the victory of May 1943 huge convoys—HX-300, for example, consisting of 167 merchant ships—had surged across the Atlantic virtually immune from attack. Britain had become an

impregnable bastion from which the final assault on the continent of Europe was on the verge of being mounted.

It has been mentioned earlier that many German hopes in the U-boat war had been pinned to the development of the Walter U-boat, a true submarine in that it would be able to operate for weeks at a time without any need to come to the surface. The project, as was said, failed to materialize, but the Walter's streamlined hull design, coupled with its great battery power, gave Dönitz an idea that might help to solve some of his present difficulties. Two new types of submarine were evolved from the original Walter design—type XXI, a U-boat of 1,600 tons capable of maintaining an underwater speed of 18 knots for an hour and a half, or 12 knots for 10 hours; and Type XXIII, a coastal U-boat with a speed of 10 knots submerged. Although the Walter hydrogen-peroxide engine was still not fully developed, snorkel breathing tubes would let them remain submerged for long periods of up to a week at a time. They were both to be of prefabricated mass construction, individual sections being built by a widely scattered number of steel firms and transhipped by inland waterways to shipyards for the installation of the internal and external fittings. Once com-

Snorkel apparatus rises from a U-boat

Type XXI submarine under construction

pleted, these sections were then to be brought to three special yards for final assembly. The wide dispersion of construction and assembly was designed to minimize any disruption by Allied bombing.

Construction was begun early in 1944. Production was to be 33 Type XXI boats a month from August 1944 and 21 Type XXIII a month from May 1944. Fortunately for the Allies these figures were never realized, for certainly the Type XXI, if it had materialized in sufficient numbers, would have proved an almost impossibly hard nut to crack. With a submerged speed greater than that of any corvette and of most frigates, the Type XXI had the ability to escape underwater from most forms of depth-charge attack. All sorts of delays and difficulties attended this attempt at mass construction, not least the carefully planned bombing of the German inland waterways along which the prefabricated sections were carried to their assembly yards. Particularly important was the breaching of the Dortmund-Ems and Mittelland Canals, both vital links in the overland route.

A more hopeful innovation was the snorkel (*Schnorchel*) breathing tube. This device enabled a submarine to run on her diesel engines while submerged at periscope depth. It had been known to the Germans since 1940, when they had seized two Dutch submarines fitted with it. It had become known to the British when a Dutch submarine escaped at the same time and reached England. But both countries ignored the invention, although toward the end of 1942 *U-448* was fitted with an experimental snorkel. Her trials, such as they were, were not followed up, and it was not until the U-boats had been defeated in the Atlantic in mid-1943 that the invention was seriously considered. Several U-boats were taken in hand to be equipped with the apparatus, and it was perhaps unfortunate that *U-264*, the first snorkel boat to be used operationally, should fall afoul of Captain Walker's support group and be sunk early in her first cruise with the new fitting.

In its early form, which was that employed by the U-boats, the snorkel had many disadvantages. If it was used in even a moderate sea that broke over the valves, the immediate result was a partial vacuum in the boat which caused great discomfort to the crew. There was also a tendency for carbon dioxide to build up, so that the crew's breathing became labored and a general feeling of lethargy resulted. This was of course a situation common to all submarines after a prolonged period of submergence, but use of the snorkel considerably accelerated the condition. Yet another difficulty was that use of the snorkel made the average speed of advance of a submarine from her base to her patrol area almost unbearably slow. During the Allied landings in France in June 1944, when all snorkel-fitted U-boats were ordered to concentrate in the English Channel in an attempt to disrupt the invasion convoys, they took nine days to reach the area from their base at Brest, the last seven days completely submerged and using their snorkels. Use of the snorkel limited their average speed of advance to

Capture of the U-505: Boarding party works on the submarine

Whaleboat passes a towline to the U-505

one and a half knots, which was not really good enough for an operational boat. Moreover, the crews were completely exhausted on arrival.

Nevertheless, the snorkel gave the U-boats some priceless advantages. No Allied radar, not even the centimetric sets, could detect the top of the snorkel tube or the small amount of periscope that appeared above water. Nor could a U-boat use her radio while submerged. So the two main methods of detection at sea, radar contact and high-frequency direction-finding, were simultaneously removed. To a large extent, this development made it virtually impossible to attack a U-boat from the air, one of the most potent forms of U-boat killing in the last year. The wholesale fitting of snorkels to U-boats was begun at the end of 1943, and by May 1944 snorkel-fitted boats were coming forward in fair numbers. They were to prove the only type of boat which could be used in the coastal waters of the English Channel, the area to which all German eyes were becoming more and more anxiously directed. For by then everyone in occupied Europe, German as well as French, Dutch and Belgian, could not fail to recognize the signs in Britain that the long-awaited invasion of Europe was imminent.

Dönitz was collecting his U-boats for the coming trial of strength, with

USS *Guadalcanal* approaches to take up the towline

large numbers held back in the Biscay and Norwegian bases until the tocsin should sound. The numbers out in the Atlantic were very considerably reduced so that as many as possible should be held ready for the emergency when it arose. It was not that Dönitz had in any way abandoned his Atlantic dreams; all he was so far prepared to do was to admit that, with the existing types of U-boats at his disposal, his dreams could only remain dreams. It was on the Type XXI that he now relied to retrieve the U-boat disaster of the past 12 months. In the U-boat War Diary, on 28 August 1944, it was remarked, "Thus the loss of the western waters would have been disastrous if our future U-boat operations depended on using the same types of boats as before. But the new boats of Type XXI, possessing very great submerged speed and submerged endurance, and capable of great diving depth, will be able to break through to the Atlantic despite concentrated opposition and to operate with success in the North Atlantic and in the remote operational areas."

But this remained no more than a hope, or a dream. When the invasion of Europe was launched across the English Channel in early June 1944, and every available U-boat drafted into the invasion area, the campaign in the Atlantic virtually came to an end. A few boats continued to patrol there, a few ships were sunk—the greatest number in any one month was five. The occasional U-boat was still destroyed in those waters, and one—U-505—was captured intact by an American hunter-killer group based on the escort carrier *Guadalcanal*. It now reposes in the Museum of Science and Industry in Chicago.

The Type XXI boats, on which so much German reliance had been placed to snatch a last-minute victory from the fires of defeat, never had a chance to demonstrate their capabilities. The first of them, *U-2511*, left Kiel on 19 March 1945. She was commanded by one of the last of the aces, Kapitänleutnant Schnee, who had been awarded the Oak Leaves of the Iron Cross as far back as 1942 for his prowess in sinking merchant ships. Eight days later *U-2511* was on her way back to her base with mechanical troubles. She sailed again on 30 April, by which time the second Type XXI was crossing the North Sea on her way to the Atlantic. Four days later, on 4 May 1945, a long signal from Dönitz, addressed to all U-boats at sea, was monitored in Britain but not immediately decrypted. With the Allied armies already in Berlin, and Germany in a state of complete collapse, there could be little doubt of its meaning. All U-boats were ordered to cease hostilities and return to their bases. Soon this instruction was followed by a general message sent in plain language, repeated every hour, ordering all of them to surface and proceed to the nearest Allied base to surrender. After five years and eight months of savage, nonstop battle, the ordeal in the Atlantic was over. Once again, merchant ships would be able to cross the oceans in peace without an ever present fear of unseen attack and destruction.

Triumphant *Guadalcanal* skipper (Captain Daniel V. Gallery) aboard U-505

12. Inshore: The Last Act

On 6 June 1944 a new U-boat campaign opened. The Allies were expecting it and ready for it. For a long time it had been obvious that the invasion, when it came, must draw to it every U-boat within range. With the Luftwaffe virtually banned from operating over the English Channel by overwhelming Allied fighter superiority, the U-boat was the only weapon with which Germany could try to hit back at the invasion convoys. Ten antisubmarine escort groups, consisting of 54 ships, with three escort carriers in attendance, guarded the western flank of the invasion area. In addition, every assault convoy had its own close surface and air escort during its passage across the Channel. The Bay of Biscay and the western approaches to the Channel were flooded with antisubmarine aircraft, flying organized patrols which guaranteed that every square mile of sea from southern Ireland to Brest was covered by at least one aircraft every half hour, day and night. Every U-boat had to get through this defense in depth before it could reach a position where it could fire a torpedo at an escorted merchant ship.

Not many succeeded. The U-boat command learned very quickly that it was suicidal for a submarine not fitted with a snorkel to attempt the passage. As soon as the Allied landings on the Normandy coast on the morning of 6 June were confirmed, a stream of U-boats left their Biscay bases, some

U.S. PBM-1 (l.) and PBM-3s on patrol

bound for the Channel invasion area, some to take up defensive positions in case the first landings proved to be a feint to disguise the real invasion elsewhere. All of them started off on the surface, making their maximum speed to their allotted stations. Between 6 and 10 June, 40 surfaced U-boats were sighted by aircraft and 24 of them attacked. They fought back furiously with their new antiaircraft armament, but six were sunk and an equal number damaged and sent limping back to their bases. Losses on such a scale forced the U-boats to submerge and use their snorkels, which slowed them to a crawl. During the remainder of June five more were destroyed in the Channel and Bay of Biscay. Five merchant ships were lost in June as a result of the U-boat onslaught.

The July results were even more dismal to U-boat headquarters. Two ships were torpedoed in the English Channel, but they cost the Germans nine U-boats. Outside the Channel three more U-boats were sunk in the transit areas from the Biscay and Norwegian bases. The Allied breakout from the invasion beachhead during August, followed by the rapid liberation of the whole of France, forced the Biscay-based U-boats to evacuate their berths and make for new ones in Norway. The loss of the Biscay ports automatically brought to an end the U-boat campaign in the Channel, and the hurried evacuation presented the opportunity for another period of intense U-boat killing. Fifteen were sunk, 12 in the Bay of Biscay and three in the Channel.

A new phase—as it turned out, the last one—of the U-boat war was about to begin. A renewal of the campaign in the Atlantic was awaiting the appearance of the Type XXI boats. Although a few of the older types were still operating there and in the more distant waters of the South Atlantic and Indian Oceans, they were now little more than a nuisance and created no real threat to the steady flow of trade convoys. The new campaign was to be waged in the coastal waters around the United Kingdom, where the snorkel was to prove a real asset. This was an area which produced new and real difficulties for the defense. Use of the snorkel precluded radar detection by either ships or aircraft. Since U-boats had no need to fill the air with radio signals, there was no opportunity to locate them by direction finding. And the waters around the United Kingdom, strewn with rocks and the wrecks of centuries, and torn with tide rips, made accurate sonar detection almost an impossibility.

One effort by the defense in this new campaign was to tighten up the coastal convoy system and increase the number of close escorts with each convoy. With the continuing military successes in Europe, and a distinct probability that the European war was approaching its end, it had been proposed to send 300 antisubmarine escorts—destroyers, frigates and corvettes—to the Far East to assist in the war against Japan, but this move was postponed until the course of the new U-boat campaign around Britain could be seen. Because great numbers of escorts were made available by this postponement, the Allies could flood the Channel and the western approaches to Britain with escort groups. In all, no fewer than 426 ships were called in to defend the convoys and to hunt the U-boats. When it is considered that the maximum number of U-boats operating in British coastal waters rarely numbered more than 50 at any one time, it may seem surprising that so many warships were required to contain them. But the number of antisubmarine ships deployed accurately reflected the very great difficulties of detection and attack.

In spite of all these problems, the U-boats were contained. The introduction of a new shortwave 3-centimeter radar which could reflect from the top of a snorkel tube was a mixed blessing; because it also reflected from any flotsam or jetsam on the surface. Nevertheless, it produced some good results. Deep minefields, laid off headlands and under some convoy routes, also swelled the number of U-boats sunk. But in the main it was the convoy escorts which kept the threat at bay.

A very early success heartened the U-boat command and provided the urge to step up the inshore campaign. During the last two days of August, U-482, commanded by Count von Matuschka, sank two merchant ships and a corvette out of a convoy off the North Irish coast. One of the ships was a tanker of over 10,000 tons. Ten days later the count attacked another convoy and sank two more ships, one of which was of more than 15,000 tons. He then returned to his base in Norway. His total cruise amounted to

2,729 miles, of which 2,473 miles were made entirely submerged, using the snorkel. The U-boat was neither sighted by aircraft nor detected by sonar throughout its cruise, in spite of having operated near a busy convoy route. This was a good indication of the difficulties which an intelligent use of the snorkel could present to the defense.

Fortunately for the Allies, this cruise proved to be an exception. None of the other 19 U-boats in British inshore waters during September achieved anything like this rate of success. One reason was certainly the many problems of reorganization following the hurried evacuation of the bases in the Bay of Biscay. This reason also explained some of the significant reduction of U-boat activity in British inshore waters during October. The submarines gradually became more active during the remainder of the year, but by now the coastal convoy system had been tightened up, with several of the support groups operating with the actual convoys instead of as independent hunter-killer groups. It was, once more, a vindication of the convoy philosophy as the only method of safeguarding seaborne trade in wartime; In its way it was a replay, with modern refinements, of the classic *guerre de course* of the 18th century.

Yet, if the campaign was being contained during the last three months of 1944, there were still some worrying features. The rate of U-boat killing had fallen dramatically below the monthly average of the last year and a half, and it was clear that the use of the snorkel had, for the time being at least, defeated all efforts by antisubmarine aircraft to detect and attack. Aircraft escorting the convoys and patrolling the main passage routes of U-boats leaving and returning to their bases had for the past 18 months been deadly, and now this means of destroying enemy submarines had largely been lost. The reduced rate of U-boat killing also meant, of course, an actual increase in the numbers of the U-boat operational fleet. In fact, the monthly intake of new construction was beginning once more to overtake the total losses, as it had done during the Allied black days of 1942 and 1943. By the end of 1944 the number of operational submarines had grown to 432; in March 1945 the U-boat fleet reached its highest operational total ever—463.

There was better cheer in contemplating the actual results of the campaign for the last four months of 1944. The U-boats had sunk 14 merchant ships in British home waters—one of them, unhappily, the troopship *Leopoldville*, sunk on Christmas Eve off Cherbourg with the loss of 800 American soldiers—and two in the Atlantic. Worldwide, 55 U-boats had been destroyed, 37 of them in British inshore waters, the Atlantic and the Arctic. But a more significant figure in this comparison of Allied and German losses was the 12,168 merchant ships which had been safely convoyed to their destination during the same four months. Even if there was comfort in these impressive figures, however, concern remained as to what might happen if the snorkel-fitted U-boats returned to the Atlantic en masse—particularly if the vastly improved Types XXI and XXIII really got into action. We know now that this new threat could not materialize because of the frustrations and delays of the prefabrication program, but we did not know it then.

At the beginning of 1945, U-boat headquarters was still optimistic about the outcome of the campaign in coastal waters. Although the Germans understood well enough that use of the snorkel showed U-boats down in their passages to the new combat areas, and then to some extent handicapped them in reaching good attacking positions once they had sighted a possible target, the fact that submarines were no longer being sunk in crippling numbers was undoubtedly encouraging. The main problem now, from Germany's point of view, was one of time. Could they hold the Allied armies in the west on the Rhine and the Soviet armies in the east on the Vistula until the U-boats came into their own again and were able to rectify the balance? That this was not an entirely unrealistic question can be corroborated by the fact that almost identical thoughts were held in London. The First Sea Lord in the British Admiralty prepared a memorandum for discussion in the Chiefs of Staff Committee which anticipated a renewal of the campaign in the Atlantic on a scale comparable with that of the early

British escort carrier *Chaser*

U.S. destroyer is damaged in a gunfire duel

months of 1943, perhaps with equally devastating losses. There was no question that the U-boats now existed in more than sufficient numbers for such a campaign, and equally there was no question that the snorkel made them much more difficult to detect. Further, the Allies still had no definite information about the progress of the Type XXI beyond the fact that some of them at least had left the training areas in the Baltic and were gathering at their Norwegian operational bases.

To Admiral Dönitz, success in the inshore campaign was a necessary prelude to a return to the broader waters of the Atlantic Ocean. The Allied armies in Europe consumed a huge volume of supplies—guns, tanks, ammunition, fuel, food and all the rest of the paraphernalia of modern war— and almost all of it had to come across the sea. If those armies were to be held clear of the Reich itself, the U-boats would need to deprive them of enough supplies to cripple their advance and thus give Germany a breathing space in which to deploy her only possible war-winning weapon, her U-boat fleet. Dönitz had no choice. A huge onslaught in the Atlantic, even if successful at the start, could mean nothing if Germany herself were obliterated in Allied advances across her borders.

Gradually, as experience and expertise in new defensive measures grew with each succeeding month, the taste of the inshore battle began to grow sour in German mouths. Allied convoy escorts and support groups became more adept in recognizing the difference between a sonar echo from a rock or an old wreck and one from a U-boat lying on the bottom. The torpedoing of a ship anywhere in these waters was followed quickly by the appearance of a support group with the time and the skill to hunt the aggressor to destruction. U-boat sinkings in inshore waters began to increase. Five were destroyed in January 1945, 10 in February, 15 in March and another 15 in April. Other sinkings occurred elsewhere, in the Atlantic, the Arctic, the Bay of Biscay and off the Norwegian coast. More devastating still were the losses inflicted in attacks on U-boat bases by British and American bombers flying from airfields in France, and the disruption of construction caused by the bombing of the main assembly yards of the prefabricated boats reduced the production of the Type XXI and XXIII boats to a trickle. Sinkings of Allied merchant ships in inshore waters reached a peak in March 1945—10 ships of 44,728 tons—a relatively tiny figure in relation to the thousands which completed their voyages in safety.

The Ludendorff bridge across the Rhine at Remagen was captured by American forces on 7 March, and on the 24th the river was crossed on a wide front further north, just south of the Netherlands border, by Field Marshal Montgomery's 21st Army Group. Time was running out fast for the Germans, but still they had failed to make the presence of their U-boats felt in the vital inshore campaign. In the end even Admiral Dönitz, whose faith in the ultimate success of his beloved U-boats had never faltered in nearly six years of war, was forced to admit that the campaign had been a failure. With its loss, all was lost, and the final curtain was being lowered on the vast European stage before any chance emerged of regrouping the U-boats in the Atlantic.

Perhaps one small star can be said to glimmer through the murk of the whole German U-boat campaign. There is no doubt that, of all the German military actions throughout the war, the U-boat campaign was the most universally detested. The savagery and ruthlessness of the attack on Allied and neutral merchant shipping was a cause of the utmost loathing among seamen of all nations, and it was in no way mitigated by the intolerant arrogance of U-boat officers and men when they were rescued from the water after the sinking of their boats. There was often a senseless disregard of human life, at times verging on atrocity. A typical example was the case of Captain Knip, master of the Dutch ship *Blitar,* torpedoed in the Atlantic in March 1943. He was in one of the ship's lifeboats when *U-631* approached to discover details of the ship sunk. In the rough sea it was impossible for the submarine to approach the lifeboats closely, and one man was ordered to swim across to *U-631.* Captain Knip was the one to volunteer, and he was duly hauled on board. He gave no information of value and was pushed back into the water, far from the lifeboats. They did their best to reach him with every man on the oars, but wind and sea were too much for them, and the captain's crew had to watch the red light on his lifejacket disappear beneath the waves. Not every U-boat captain acted with such callousness, of course, but there is always a tendency to believe that the actions of one reflected the actions of all in this vicious campaign. Many U-boat captains were honorable and humane men, even if their trade were a despicable one.

Yet the small star still glimmers, if only in consideration of the resoluteness of the U-boat crews even when they must have realized that defeat was only just around the corner. Right up to the end they never gave up the fight, never failed willingly to accept the sacrifices which Dönitz thrust upon them. Finally, in his desperation to achieve the breathing space which Germany needed, he used them recklessly, and many U-boats perished in a senseless pursuit. The figures tell the story. Of a total strength of just over 39,000 officers and men who manned the U-boats throughout the war, a little more than 28,000 were killed or drowned, a much greater percentage of loss than recorded by any other service in any nation. However detestable their acts in Allied eyes, however ruthless their mode of warfare, there has to be some admiration for resolution and fortitude such as that. It may be a faint star, but it is still a star.

It is impossible to calculate the total loss of merchant seamen throughout this long and bitter campaign, for there are no accurate figures available for all the neutral countries whose ships sailed in Allied convoys. Many neutral ships were sunk, many of their crews were lost. Perhaps the British figures may reflect the losses suffered by the other concerned na-

171

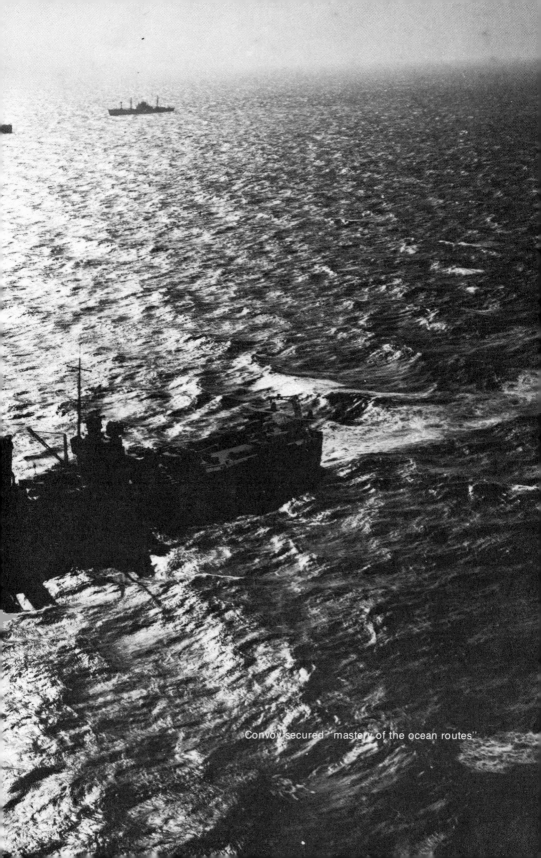
Convoy secured "mastery of the ocean routes"

tions, for the U-boats sank ships regardless of the flags under which they sailed. From the total of British merchant seamen of about 185,000, no fewer than 32,052 lost their lives in this groping underwater campaign —nearly one man out of every five. And there were of course noncombatants, men—and a few women accompanying their husbands on board——whose calling in life caught them in a war which was not of their making. No medals or promotions came their way; they were not trained for war; the glamor of war, such as it may be, passed them by. Yet the war as a whole could never have been won without their courage and dedication, their willingness and often eagerness to go back again and again and face the continuing menace of modern submarine warfare. If war makes heroes, then all of these merchant seamen were among them.

One of the last words about this whole campaign should perhaps go in praise of the work of the rescue ships, which from June 1942 sailed with almost all the Atlantic and Arctic convoys. Only in exceptional cases—when no rescue ship was available, either through storm damage or because of loss by enemy action—did a convoy sail without one in attendance. Always they were little ships, trawlers or similar, with a medical team on board and such few comforts as could be carried to help those rescued from the sea and directly from torpedoed ships. Twenty-nine of these small ships were commissioned during the war, and between them they made no fewer than 796 transoceanic voyages. They picked up 4,183 survivors, men who would otherwise have had little or no chance of escaping death, and brought them home in safety. Six of the rescue ships were torpedoed and sunk by U-boats, an overall rate of loss far greater than that in the convoyed merchant ships which they served. Their crews, too, are surely among the unsung heroes of the ocean war.

"Amid the torrent of violent events," wrote Winston Churchill of this great war, "one anxiety reigned supreme. Battles might be won or lost, enterprises might succeed or miscarry, territories might be gained or quitted, but dominating all our powers to carry on the war, or even to keep ourselves alive, lay our mastery of the ocean routes and the free approach and entry to our ports."

Just so, or, as the great Duke of Wellington wrote of the Battle of Waterloo 130 years previously, "It had been a damned nice thing—the nearest run thing you ever saw in your life."

In Context

As *Decision at Sea: The Convoy Escorts* makes plain, the battle that flared and flamed in the Atlantic Ocean from the first day of the war to the last was as close as any one aspect of the global struggle could have come to being vital and essential to the victory, whichever side was to be the victor. The Allies won the battle, and so they won the war. It is not that simple, of course—but no one doubts that, had the battle gone against the Allies, the shape of the war would have been vastly different. Even before entering the war, the United States was, as President Roosevelt proclaimed, the "great arsenal of democracy." Munitions and supplies went across the ocean to Britain and the Soviet Union. First matériel—and then, from the beginning of 1942, men in growing tens of thousands.

The particular problem faced by the United States in World War II was that it was engaged in fighting on two fronts that were on opposite sides of the world—and each was thousands of miles from the great arsenal and training camp. There was, although it is not so called, a Battle of the Pacific, too—a battle of extremely long lifelines and uniquely difficult logistic problems.

Some historians, in fact, put the beginning of the war on that side of the world—in the summer of 1937, when fighting broke out between the Japanese and the Chinese (and this fighting itself was actually part of a story that had been evolving since 1931). But the usual date for the coming of the war is 1 September 1939, when the Germany of Adolf Hitler

175

launched its invasion of Poland. It was a quick, victorious campaign for the German armies. And in 1940, while Japan pursued her goals in China, the Germans swept through Europe in an amazing march of conquest: Denmark, Norway, the Netherlands, Luxembourg, Belgium and, to the world's shock, France. But the Germans could not cross water; they could not conquer Britain without control of the air and thus of the sea. That control the Battle of Britain, in the summer of 1940, denied them. The war in Europe would go on.

While these events, and others traced in this book, were unfolding, the Americans were watching Asia with deep concern. The Japanese were going about the establishment of a "Greater East Asia Co-Prosperity Sphere"—the extension of the Japanese Empire to Burma, Indochina, Malaya and the Netherlands East Indies. This expansion was viewed in Washington as a threat to American security as well as to friends of the United States. But Britain, extended to her limit, had little force in Asia with which to oppose the Japanese advance.

Then came 7 December 1941, and Pearl Harbor. The United States was now an active belligerent, alongside Britain and Russia. In accordance with previously agreed-upon strategy, the main American effort was first directed against Germany—considered the most potent of the Axis partners. This book has made reference to the consequences of this strategy—the campaigns in North Africa and the Mediterranean, and the invasion of northwest Europe in 1944. But contrary to Japanese expectations, there was, in early 1942, a significant American naval presence in the Pacific (see the Men and Battle book *Carrier Victory: The Air War in the Pacific*). Japanese moves southward were checked in the Battle of the Coral Sea. In June came the pivotal American defeat of the Japanese fleet at Midway. It was, surprisingly early, the turning point in the Pacific war and thus one of the great turning points of World War II as a whole. The United States could now take the offensive, which it did in August, landing in the Solomon Islands. The long march across the Pacific was on. It led to New Guinea, to the Gilberts, the Marshalls, Saipan, Tinian, Guam and the Philippines. Then, at the beginning of April 1945, American forces landed on Okinawa. While this battle was being fought, Hitler's Germany, crushed between the Anglo-American and Soviet armies and battered by Allied bombing, breathed its last, a few days after the suicide of its Führer. The bombing campaign is described in detail in *The Men Who Bombed the Reich*, another of the Men and Battle books.

On winning the battle of Okinawa, at the doorstep of Japan, Allied leaders looked to an invasion of the Home Islands—a campaign that would have been one of blood and horrors. But both sides were spared it. Already isolated, with fire raids demolishing her cities, Japan received the two atomic blows. After Hiroshima and Nagasaki, there could only be an end to the war.

For Further Reading

BEESLY, PATRICK. *Very Special Intelligence.* Garden City, N.Y.: Doubleday, 1978.

BRENNECKE, HANS J. *The Hunters and the Hunted.* New York: Norton, 1958.

BUSCH, HAROLD. *U-boats at War.* New York: Ballantine, 1956.

CHALMERS, W. S. *Max Horton and the Western Approaches.* London: Hodder & Stoughton, 1954.

CREIGHTON, SIR KENELM. *Convoy Commodore.* London: Kimber, 1956.

DOENITZ, KARL. *Memoirs: Ten Years and Twenty Days.* Cleveland and New York: World, 1959.

FARAGO, LADISLAS. *The Tenth Fleet.* New York: Obolensky, 1962.

GRETTON, SIR PETER. *Convoy Escort Commander.* London: Cassell, 1964.

———. *Crisis Convoy* [HX-231]. London: Davies, 1974.

KEMP, PETER. *Key to Victory: The Triumph of British Sea Power in World War II.* Boston: Little, Brown, 1957.

MACINTYRE, DONALD. *The Battle of the Atlantic.* New York: Macmillan, 1961.

———. *U-boat Killer.* New York: Norton, 1957.

MORISON, SAMUEL ELIOT. *History of United States Naval Operations in World War II* (particularly vols. I and X). Boston: Little, Brown, 1947–62.

POOLMAN, KENNETH. *Escort Carrier, 1941–1945.* London: Allan, 1972.

RIESENBERG, F. *Sea War: The Story of the U.S. Merchant Marine in World War II.* New York: Rinehart, 1956.

ROBERTSON, TERENCE. *The Golden Horseshoe.* London: Evans, 1955.

————. *Walker, R.N.: The Story of Captain Frederick John Walker*. London: Evans, 1956.

ROHWER, JÜRGEN. *The Critical Convoy Battles of March 1943* [HX-229/SC-122]. Annapolis: Naval Institute Press, 1973.

ROSKILL, S. W. *The Secret Capture* [U-110]. London: Collins, 1959.

————. *The War at Sea, 1939–1945*. London: H.M. Stationery Office, 1954–61.

SCHOFIELD, B. B., and MARTYN, L. F. *The Rescue Ships*. Edinburgh: Blackwood, 1968.

SCHULL, JOSEPH. *The Far Distant Ships*. Ottawa: Cloutier, 1952.

SETH, RONALD. *The Fiercest Battle* [ONS-5]. New York: Norton, 1962.

SLESSOR, SIR JOHN. *The Central Blue*. New York: Praeger, 1957.

TUCKER, G. N. *The Naval Service of Canada*. Ottawa: Government Printing Office, 1952.

WATSON-WATT, SIR ROBERT. *The Pulse of Radar*. New York: Dial, 1959.

Index

WS, 59
see also convoy escorts; German navy; merchant shipping
Cook, James, 2, 3, 4-6

Dagabur, 82
Dasher, 104
Denmark, 26, 34
Denmark Strait, 16
depth charges, 10, 24, 38-39, 46, 50, 54, 93-94, 106
Dianthus, 61
Dönitz, Karl:
  Athenia sinking and, 8
  on Battle of the Atlantic, 127
  command role of, 20, 22-23, 27, 30, 33, 36-37, 116, 141, 161, 171
  defeat and, 161, 170
  Hitler and, 38, 67, 141
  intelligence activities and, 23, 55-56, 91, 101, 103, 148, 151
  naval operations planned by, 20, 24-25, 27-28, 42, 47, 103, 111, 120-121, 146-148, 149-152, 155, 157,160-161
  newly trained crews and, 103, 111
  surface tactics of, 27-28
  on U.S. coastal attacks, 48-49
  victory formula of, 22, 24, 47, 49, 97
  War Diary entries of, 62, 120, 122
  "wolf-pack" tactics of, 27, 28, 42-43, 93, 98-99, 100-102, 119-120, 149-151
Duke of York, 141, 142

Eagle, 82
Edinburgh, 71
Eisenhower, Dwight D., 134
Electra, 6
English Channel, 158, 160, 163, 164
Enigma machine and system, 23-24, 56-57, 100, 118, 148, 151, 152-153
Escort, 6
escorts, *see* convoy escorts

Faeroe Islands, 1, 34, 63, 151
Fame, 6
FAT, 90
Fegen, Edward Fogarty, 16
Fink, 120
Flower-class corvettes, 12, 29
Focke-Wulf 200 Condor, 31
Foxer, 148, 149
France, 26, 30, 164
  see also Normandy invasion
Fraser, Sir Bruce, 141
Friedrich Eckoldt, 139
Furious, 82

German air force, *see* Luftwaffe
German navy, 36, 56, 72, 89-90
  Athenia sinking and, 8, 14
  convoy JW-51 B and, 136-140
  convoy PQ-17 and, 71-78
  convoy PQ-18 and, 130-134
  plans for war in, 11-12, 13, 14
  surface vessels of, 13, 14, 16, 18-19, 67, 68-69, 72, 74-75, 130-131, 134, 136-140, 141-142

U-boat headquarters of, 22-23, 30, 56, 91, 110, 123, 148, 149, 163-164, 165-166
  see also Dönitz, Karl; U-boats
Germany:
  Allied advances on (1945), 167-170
  Athenia sinking and, 6-8, 14
  conquests of (1939-40), 26, 176
  naval planning of, 11, 13
  Soviet Union invaded by, 35
  U.S. war entry and, 47-48
Gibraltar, 15, 33, 117
Gibraltar Straits, 33
Gneisenau, 13, 18-19, 67
Golden Comb, 72, 132
Göring, Hermann, 67
Great Britain, 35, 49, 50, 176
  anticipation of war in, 2-4, 14
  Athenia sinking and, 7-8, 14
  coastal waters of, 15, 30, 160, 165-167, 170
  dependence on shipping of, 9-10, 22, 49, 59, 97, 126, 174
  invasion buildup in, 22, 87, 155-157
  preparation for war in, 7, 10-11, 12, 16
  shipbuilding in, 8, 12, 16, 28, 35, 38, 41, 49, 52, 97
  U.S. and, 6, 37, 46, 66, 97-98
Greenland, 37
Greenland air gap, 59, 92, 113
Greer, 37
Gretton, Peter, 113, 114, 119, 121-122
Guadalcanal, 161
Guadalcanal Island, 134

Hagenuk receiver, 148
Hague Convention, 1, 7, 14
Hamilton, L. H. K., 75
Hannover, see Audacity
"happy time," *see* U-boats
Harvester, 99
Hawker Hurricane, 32, 35, 131, 132
Hawkins, Arthur, 17-18
Heathcote, R., 94
Hedgehog, 38-39, 106
HF/DF ("huff-duff"), 90, 103, 116, 117, 124, 160
Hipper, 72, 74, 130-131, 134, 136-139, 140
Hitler, Adolf, 6, 7, 11, 12, 13, 14, 27, 28, 31, 38, 67, 69, 72, 75, 131
Horton, Sir Max, 63, 94, 104, 114, 117, 124
Hunt-class destroyers, 12
"hunter-killer" groups, 152-153
Hydra, 56, 57, 58

ice and snow, hazards of, 143-144
Iceland, 34-35, 37, 47, 51
Impulsive, 134
Indian Ocean, 85, 165
Indomitable, 82
intelligence operations:
  British, 23-24, 43, 55-58, 91, 100, 110, 118, 123, 148, 151
  German, 23, 55-56, 82, 91, 94, 101, 103, 117, 148, 151
international law, 1, 10, 11, 12, 14
Ireland, 2, 15, 51
Italy, 79-80, 82, 83, 84